Gender Consciousness and Privilege

Gender Consciousness and Privilege offers an innovative new framework for understanding the role of gender in education. Based on the results of a two-year study of three schools undergoing major organizational changes as they prepared for coeducation, it promotes understanding of the role gender plays in influencing change in a high school.

The book focuses on the impact of education on both sexes, placing responsibility for creating gender-fair environments on how educators organize their work and how they create environments for learning. The following questions are addressed:

- What does gender consciousness mean for creating fair and gender-affirmative learning environments?
- How does the level of gender consciousness affect the culture of schools and the experience of students in different gender settings?
- What does this teach us about the education of females and males?
- How do single sex and coeducational contexts influence the education process for young people?

The authors examine how assumptions about gender and male privilege are embedded in the culture, the curriculum, the interpersonal interactions inside and outside the classroom, and the psychology of the students. They discover that the combination of leadership, staff, curricular awareness, and an understanding of gender-fair and gender-affirmative practices greatly influence institutional environment.

The authors work with students and professionals at all levels of the educational system. **Celeste M. Brody**, **Nancy G. Nagel**, **Glennellen Pace** and **Patricia Schmuck** are on the faculty of Lewis and Clark College. **Susan Randles Moscato** is an Associate Professor in the School of Nursing at the University of Portland. **Penny Poplin Gosetti** teaches at the University of Toledo. **Kasi Allen Fuller** is an educational consultant and evaluator.

Gender Consciousness and Privilege

Celeste M. Brody, Kasi Allen Fuller, Penny Poplin Gosetti, Susan Randles Moscato, Nancy G. Nagel, Glennellen Pace, and Patricia Schmuck

London and New York

First published 2000
by Falmer Press
11 New Fetter Lane, London EC4P 4EE

Simultaneously published in the USA and Canada
by Falmer Press
Garland Inc., 19 Union Square West, New York, NY 10003

Falmer Press is an imprint of the Taylor & Francis Group

© 2000 Brody, Fuller, Gosetti, Moscato, Nagel, Pace, Schmuck

Typeset in Times by Taylor & Francis Books Ltd
Printed and bound in Great Britain by MPG Books Ltd, Chatham

British Library Cataloguing in Publication Data
A catalogue record for this book is available from the British Library

Library of Congress Cataloging in Publication Data
Gender consciousness and privilege / Celeste M. Brody [et al.]
    p.   cm.
    Includes bibliographical references and index.
    ISBN 0–750–70999–5 (hard: alk. paper). – ISBN 0–750–70998–7
    (pbk. :alk. paper)
    1. Coeducation–United States Case studies. 2. Educational
    equalization– United States Case studies. 3. Catholic
    Church–Education–United States Case studies.   I. Brody, Celeste M.
    LB3066.G46   1999
    306.43–dc21   99–28035

ISBN 0–750–70998–7 (pbk)
ISBN 0–750–70999–5 (hbk)

Contents

Contents

vi

Illustrations

Tables

Figures

Acknowledgments

We are grateful to the following people who participated in initiating this research in 1991–1992. Mary Henning-Stout, Professor of Counseling Psychology, Lewis and Clark College, worked as a consultant to an all-female high school in our study that moved to coeducation; her work with the school provided us with invaluable data. She also served on the planning committee and helped us conceptualize the project. Sorca O'Connor, Professor of Educational Foundations, Portland State University, conducted interviews with the faculty, administrators, and staff at an all-male high school in our study that became coeducational. Ken Kempner, Associate Professor, University of Oregon, met with the young men's focus group, participated in some of the planning committee meetings, and also conducted interviews. We also appreciate the work of Amy Beacom, Ryan Farr, Susan Hopp, Mary Lind, Sarah Schacker, and Wendy Whittemore who gathered classroom data at all three schools.

We are particularly indebted to the Special Interest Group (SIG), Research on Women in Education of the American Educational Research Association (AERA). We gave numerous papers at the annual meetings of both the SIG and AERA and the inspiring and helpful discussions held at those meetings were invaluable.

We also appreciate the grant received from the David and Loa Mason Charitable Trust. Kirsten Truman, Assistant in the Educational Administration Program at Lewis and Clark College, was very helpful in administering the grant, juggling our various schedules, and responding to the differing needs of the seven authors. We are grateful for the assistance provided by the Graduate School of Professional Studies at Lewis and Clark College.

We thank Carole Shmurak and Jo Sanders who reviewed our work and gave us feedback. Richard Schmuck edited the entire book and helped us to clarify our meanings where we had written obtusely; we are grateful for the good use of his red pen.

Acknowledgments

Finally, we are grateful to the teachers and administrators in our study who must remain nameless to protect their anonymity. Their thoughtfulness, willingness to be part of the study, and cooperation were greatly appreciated. We are in debt and hope our study will be valuable to them.

Introduction

After thirty-two years as an elite, all-male school, Xavier Preparatory High School[1] changed its educational mission. The school decided to enroll young women. Xavier's decision to become coeducational affected the educational environment of a large Catholic diocese including two other single-sex sister schools, one that also became coeducational, and the other that affirmed its commitment to a continued mission of single-sex education. The decision also provided a serendipitous opportunity to study gender within the context of single-sex and coeducational settings.

This book is about the discoveries we made in studying those schools; what we learned about society's collective gender consciousness and the unidentified and unspoken assumptions about male privilege. It also explores how that collective consciousness permeates the experiences of educators and students in both single-sex and coeducational schools. This book is not about taking a stand on whether single-sex or coeducational schools are better for females. Although single-sex and coeducational schools are quite different, we do not intend to judge the schools in our study nor weigh the advantages or disadvantages of single-sex or coeducational schooling. We believe that the degree to which participants in a school are aware of assumptions about gender and male privilege does influence the "goodness" of a school. We also know, however, that sex is only one variable among many that make up the culture of the school. Patricia Schmuck's daughter, Julie, at age 16 understood the multiplicity of variables that make up a school. Julie was transplanted from an alternative public junior high school in Eugene, Oregon, to a Flemish-speaking, Catholic, all-girls' high school in Belgium. When her mother asked her, "How do you like going to an all-girls' school?" Julie replied, "Mother, everything is so different I can't tell whether being all-female makes a difference or not."

In this book we describe a two-year, multifaceted study that sought to understand the role that gender played in schools facing the changes and challenges of a transition from single-sex to coeducation. The distinctive period of change experienced by the three Catholic high schools we studied provided us the opportunity to explore gender consciousness and privilege in favorable settings. All three of these schools are considered excellent schools; they are academically sound, they have sensitive and caring staff, they treat students with respect, and they are committed to helping students develop a public-service conscience. These are good schools for students, for faculty, for administrators, and for parents. Each school experiences a high level of commitment from parents, supportive alumni and friends, and a strong sense of community. We hope they can provide lessons for all schools.

Context of the Study: Field Sites

Each of the high schools in this study faced decisions about remaining single-sex or becoming coeducational in the late 1980s.[2] Xavier, the remaining all-male school in the Jesuit (Society of Jesus) Province, decided to become coeducational starting in 1993. Grove Catholic High School, formerly St. Theresa of the Grove, an all-female high school, decided to admit boys starting in 1991, and St. Elizabeth's Academy reaffirmed its decision to be a school for females only.

Xavier Preparatory High School

Xavier is a Jesuit school and inexorably linked to the tradition of Jesuits in America. According to Bryk et al. (1993), the Jesuits had an early and important influence in American education. They established schools in the 1600s and the curriculum, *The Ratio Studiorum*, a focus on the value of classical study, the transmission of the accumulated wisdom of Western culture, and individual contemplation, influenced the American secondary school curriculum.

Xavier admitted its first freshman class in the 1950s. Located on a former dairy farm near a metropolitan center, its first "primitive and unfinished" school was staffed by three Jesuit priests and two Jesuit scholastics. When the first class graduated, the student body had quadrupled in numbers and the campus was taking shape. The student body grew by another 150 and maintained that number for the next few decades. Many families sent their sons to Xavier and their daughters to St. Elizabeth's; they were considered academically comparable schools. After thirty years as a successful college preparatory school (close to 98 percent of the students attend college following graduation) with winning sports teams, the enrollment declined precariously in the 1980s to its lowest enrollment since its early years of operation. Xavier's Board of Trustees and alumni were greatly concerned with the decline in enrollment as well as with the population demographics that showed a decrease in the number of children of school age in the surrounding parochial schools and an economic slump in the state. At the same time, parents, community, and alumni were beginning to favor admitting girls to the previously all-male schools. Xavier had remained all-male and alumni and parents had been asking, "Why can't my daughter get the same Jesuit education as my son?" Strong, active, and aging alumni argued that the natural situation is for men and women to live and work together. In this changing world, the Jesuit ideal of *leadership education* for men became important for daughters as well. Riordan (1990) suggests that the justification of coeducation as the "natural situation" often appears after the economic factor rears its head. Institutions begin to change the conventional wisdom and discard or modify values on which the institution was based. In the case of Xavier, the issue of coeducation began to be explored along with the concern of how to apply the Ignatian pedagogy to "men *and women* for others."

Grove Catholic High School

St. Theresa of the Grove was founded in the first decade of this century as a residential school for boys and girls by a Congregation of Sisters newly arrived in the northwestern United States. Located in a bustling, emerging, suburban town, the school grew over the years to include a coeducational preschool, kindergarten, elementary, and junior high program. Traditionally, the high school remained an all-female school and was well supported by loyal alumni and families. During the late 1970s and 1980s, the high school experienced a marked decline in enrollment to a record low number of students and rumors abounded throughout the community that the school might close. With Xavier's decision to become coeducational, the faculty, members of the religious order and school community decided to change to coeducation as well. In order to attract young men, they changed the school name from the female St. Theresa to the neutral designation of Grove Catholic High School.

St. Elizabeth's Academy

St. Elizabeth's Academy is one of the oldest high schools in the region. Founded in the mid-1800s by a Congregation of Sisters, its mission was to "encourage full human development through education in faith." Located in an urban setting, St. Elizabeth's always has been an all-girls' school. The Sisters believed in the power of education as exemplified by their foundress, that "to educate a person is to educate a family, and regenerate a nation, and a world." With education, women could become leaders and change the world.

St. Elizabeth's has been awarded a national exemplary school award, and the distinguished school award for exceptional use of technology in the curriculum. Unlike Xavier and St. Theresa's, the enrollment at St. Elizabeth's remained steady through the 1970s and 1980s. As Xavier altered its mission to embrace coeducation, St. Elizabeth's reaffirmed its unique mission in the diocese to remain an all-female college preparatory school.

The Coeducation Decision

Consistent with Riordan's (1990) analysis that the typical impetus for coeducation is economic, Xavier's decision to move to coeducation was based on the fact that the pool of male applicants was steadily declining during the 1980s. Table 0.1 shows the key events that occurred in the change from single-sex to coeducation that began in the late 1980s. In March of 1987, Xavier's Board of Trustees approved a study to determine if Xavier should become a coeducational school. They proposed fall, 1990, as an initial date for Xavier to become coeducational. The other Catholic high schools in the metropolitan area, particularly St. Elizabeth's, registered an immediate and concerned response: Does one school have the right to change its composition for its own reasons? And at what cost to others?

Representatives of St. Elizabeth's, St. Theresa's, Xavier, and other Catholic high schools in the metropolitan area marshaled two responses to this question. First, St. Elizabeth's and St. Theresa's agreed to join with Xavier to support a regional study to survey a random sample of parochial grade school and high school students regarding the coeducational issue and the nature of the three schools. Second, in June, 1987, the Catholic Archbishop appointed a collaborative committee facilitated by a nun to mediate the situation and assist all the area Catholic high schools to reach consensus about the coeducational issue.

The all-girls' schools found disturbing the findings of the regional study presented in October, 1987. The researchers who conducted the study concluded that if Xavier became a coeducational school, St. Elizabeth's would lose one-third of its students and St. Theresa's would be forced to close due to declining enrollment. They predicted no new influx of students entering the Catholic high schools; rather, they saw a rearrangement of the current and prospective students.

The collaborative committee began work in the fall with dialogue among the metropolitan area Catholic high schools intended to reach consensus regarding the coeducation decision at Xavier and to establish a timetable for the transition. The Archbishop gave the directive that he would not approve a plan upon which the schools had not agreed. Participants at these meetings included the principals, presidents, representatives, and chairs of the Board of Trustees at the respective schools.

Persons involved in the meetings remember them as "painful collaborations." One reported, "We had an incredible set of good people all with a role to play" and "it was amazing that we were able to come to resolution." It was apparent that Xavier exercised a privileged position within the Catholic community – it had originally planned to chart a course of action that was favorable to it with little thought to the consequences of that decision for the other schools. Participants believed that Xavier had the power to make a decision to become a coeducational institution, and as someone stated in a meet-ing, "Nobody can really tell Xavier what to do." But

Table 0.1 Key Events in the Change from Single-Sex to Coeducation within a Catholic Archdiocese

Year	Event
1987	Xavier Preparatory decides to become a coeducational high school.
	Bishop of the diocese convenes study team to determine impact of this decision on single-sex sister high schools: St. Theresa of the Grove and St. Elizabeth's.
1988	Xavier agrees to take 5 years before changing to coeducation.
	St. Elizabeth's affirms single-sex mission.
	St. Theresa decides to become coed and change name to Grove Catholic High School.
1989–1990	Xavier Prep begins a capital campaign to double student enrollment. Faculty begins plans for coeducation.
1991	Grove High admits boys to freshmen class only as they transition to full coeducation.
	Study team member begins holding female focus group at Grove Catholic High School.
1992	Study team forms to follow transition of Xavier; data collection begins.
1993	Data collection intensifies at all three schools, particularly Xavier.
	Females are admitted to Xavier as 50% of freshmen class and enrollment increases from 400 students to nearly 800 students.
1994	Transition to coeducation complete at Grove Catholic High School.
	Transition continues at Xavier with enrollments increasing each year for 50/50 gender balanced classes.
1995	Study team begins data interpretation.

another participant recounted, "Xavier had the right to go coeducational, but a Catholic mediating force made that impossible" without the consent of all concerned. Catholic values and family connections influenced the decision making – too many families had ties to each of the affected schools, and too much was at stake for the institutions that were not Jesuit. As a participant recounted, there was clear recognition that "you don't just put the screws to someone else also trying to do good work." Thus, the representatives of these schools determined to work in collaboration within the committee to set the coeducation decision in motion and to develop a timetable that would be advantageous to all of the schools.

The dialogue among the schools continued throughout the academic year. Key negotiated factors revolved around the timetable for Xavier's transition to coeducational schooling. St. Elizabeth's was particularly concerned that it would have the time to solidify its support base, increase its enrollment, and communicate its mission as an all-female school. This was important because Xavier and St. Elizabeth's traditionally had drawn students from the same families and were both college preparatory schools. St. Theresa's requested time to develop a clear mission that would help determine its future.

Demographics also played a central role in the timetable decision. Population studies indicated that in 1987, the enrollment of 6th, 7th, and 8th graders in local parochial schools was low. In contrast, grades 3–5 had larger classes coming along.

Finally, after hours of dialogue the schools developed a plan. At the May, 1988 meeting of the collaborative committee, Xavier made the following proposal: If there is consensus for the 1993–1994 school year, with Xavier converting all four grades at once, Xavier will ask its board for a response to that proposal. The proposal was forwarded to and approved by the respective boards of each school and, finally, the Archbishop. Xavier would become coeducational in the fall of 1993, three years after it initially had planned to make that move. That was the negotiated compromise and a welcomed time extension for the other schools.

Following the process pioneered by Xavier two years earlier, the representative of St. Theresa's met with the other Catholic high schools in the region to reach a consensus about St. Theresa's becoming coeducational. Consensus was achieved after only one meeting, and the Archbishop gave permission for St. Theresa's also to become a coeducational school, starting with one class per year in the fall of 1991. Early in the transition concern was expressed about the school's name, "Guys don't want to go to a girls' school," so the school's name was changed from St. Theresa's of the Grove to Grove Catholic High School (which is the name we use throughout the text). At the same time, St. Elizabeth's reaffirmed its tradition of remaining an all-female college preparatory school.

The decision to admit women affected Xavier dramatically. The coeducation plan included doubling the school enrollment by admitting females to all four years and recruiting actively from Catholic and public feeder schools and families with ties to Xavier and the Jesuit tradition. The school launched a major building and fund-raising campaign. Activities were started to facilitate the hiring of more female staff and to decide on how best to provide an easy transition for the young women. One example that captures the scope of these decisions involves Xavier's reputation for having an unusually strong athletics program. In fact, athletics are almost synonymous with Xavier, and include football, swimming, track and field, tennis, golf, and basketball. Equal access for girls to the benefits of a Xavier education required that they have comparable sports opportunities. Thus, transition plans included the decision to have the same number of sports for girls (girls' volleyball would be comparable to boys' football), and to open a coed Xavier with varsity-level girls' teams, even though the number of sophomore, junior and senior girls would be considerably fewer than the 50–50 freshmen class. The significance of that decision was quickly realized as female freshmen and transfer students – particularly from St. Elizabeth's and Grove – were attracted to Xavier.

The decision to admit young men also dramatically affected Grove, the former St. Theresa's. In contrast to Xavier's five-year transition plan, Grove had one year to prepare for its first freshmen coed class. A modest capital campaign was launched to provide additions to the athletic center, add men's restrooms and enhance the academic and athletic programs. A well-known coach was recruited and hired for the boys' basketball team amongst great publicity and fanfare despite the fact that the freshmen class did not include enough boys to make a basketball team.

The Decision and State Tax Reform

During the five-year transition to coeducation, a set of local events altered Xavier's initial economic reason for integration. Following passage of a property tax limitation measure in 1990, more people became attracted to private and parochial education as the public schools faced reductions in funding (a reduction of 1.5 percent each year for a five-year period). At the same time, classes grew larger, special programs were cut, and many parents of school children chose not to believe the educators who said they were doing more with less. Students began fleeing public schools for private education. In addition to the families that had traditionally attended Catholic schools, these schools began to attract many students from families who were concerned with the loss of funding in the public schools and wanted to ensure good schooling for their children.

Generalizations to Public Schools

The schools in our study were Catholic. We believe, however, that educators in public schools can learn from studies of gender consciousness and privilege in Catholic schools just as we believe that educators in private schools can learn from similar studies in public schools. It seems to be popular, however, to believe that because Catholic schools have the luxury of selecting their students they can achieve higher levels of student academic achievement. We have to acknowledge the power of self-selection in creating strong

7

school cultures and that public high schools usually do not have such strong and consistent cultures that they control. Public schools take all students who come to their doors.

At the same time, considerable debate and very different research findings exist today than existed in the 1970s and 1980s about achievement differences between private (primarily Catholic) and public schools. Researchers (Lee, 1997; LePore and Warren, 1997) have concluded that much has changed in American public and private schools over the past two decades. All schools are becoming increasingly diverse. Actually, more differences probably exist today between public high schools of different sizes, geographic location, and student demographics than exist between public and private schools serving similar student populations. The seminal issue today is understanding the effect of the organizational culture on females and males, and how educational practice might change to implement "best practices" for young women. We believe knowledge derived from studying the three schools we focused upon can contribute to stronger and more equitable practices for females and males.

Conclusion

As educators, we must strive to understand our school cultures and use that understanding to develop "best" and equitable practices for our students. In this book, we invite educators interested in developing that understanding to reflect on the following questions:

- How does gender consciousness and privilege affect the culture of schools and the experience of students in different gendered environments?
- What do educators need to know about the education of females and males? How can we be assured our daughters and sons are developing to their full potential?
- What does gender consciousness mean for creating truly equitable learning environments?

These are the questions that evolved from our study; they reflect the changes in our learnings and understandings about gender that emerged as we gathered our data, discussed and argued over our collective and personal meanings of those data, and dealt with contradictory and paradoxical findings. We hope that the findings from our study presented in the following chapters will provide guidance in answering these important questions.

Chapter 1 describes the research design and methods with which we began our journey of discovery. It also introduces some of the research and theory about Catholic education, single-sex education and coeducation, gender consciousness, and privilege that helped us understand our discoveries. Chapter 2 describes the faculty members of an all-male high school, and what they believed would change when the school became coeducational. Chapter 3 presents an in-depth examination of the classrooms and pedagogies of three teachers, each teacher from a different discipline and a different school. We show how their beliefs about gender and the culture of the school influenced their pedagogy. Chapter 4 discusses students' perceptions and expectations of their school and how those perceptions and expectations were influenced by the gendered cultures of single-sex and coeducational settings. Chapter 5 addresses the issue of gender consciousness in the curriculum through a focus on mathematics education in the three high schools. Chapter 6 discusses the strengths and the challenges of conducting effective feminist action research. Chapter 7 concludes the book by proposing a framework that will guide educators to levels of critical transformation that truly may be empowering for students and suggesting how that framework might inform policy and practice.

Notes

1   All names of schools, teachers, and other participants in this study have been changed for this book.
2   The history of the schools, based on archival material and personal experience, was written by a member of the Board of Trustees at Xavier who also was an active parent at St. Elizabeth's. This author's intimate experience of Catholic education has been an invaluable resource to the research team.

1   Studying Gender Consciousness and Privilege

Vigorous debate about the benefits of single-sex and coeducational schools for females and males has occurred internationally since the 1980s. We joined the debate because of the research opportunity provided by two Catholic high schools in the same geographical area that were changing from single-sex to coeducation; one female and one male. Another Catholic high school in the same geographical area that reaffirmed its commitment to remain all-female provided a comparable single-sex school.

Evolution of the Study

Our research began in 1992, the year prior to Xavier's change to coeducation. Administrators at Xavier, St. Elizabeth's, and Grove had completed their administrative licensure work with Patricia Schmuck. The Xavier principal asked for consultative help to guide Xavier's transition from a single-sex to a coeducational school. The principal expected the presence of young women would change the Xavier culture, forcing everyone to change the way they educated young people. Patricia disagreed. She argued the introduction of young women in the school would not easily change the school's culture nor pedagogical style of teaching and learning; in five years she expected Xavier to be much the same, except with young women present. On the other hand, she argued, Grove, which had just admitted young men to its freshman class, would be different; the presence of young men would change the culture and pedagogy of the previously all-female school.

That conversation led to others and in May, 1992, Patricia invited administrators from the three schools and researchers interested in gender issues from three universities to discuss the possibilities of conducting a naturalistic study. The first meeting of the planning committee included the male principal and male rector of Xavier, the female principal of St. Elizabeth's, two female teachers from Xavier, and ten academics (including the seven authors) from three different universities.

It was a unique opportunity for study; no comparable research existed in the United States. Most private single-sex schools passed out of favor after the Second World War and, since the founding of our U.S. public educational system, educators have held the unquestioned assumption that coeducation was the most desirable configuration for *all* students (Riordan, 1990). We, the researchers, were excited about what we would learn from the three school settings as they moved through the experience of coeducation, and educators at the school sites were pleased about assistance they might receive through a collaborative research agenda. The fact that the three Catholic schools were a close alliance meant that the student populations were relatively homogeneous.

Our planning meetings were friendly and supportive, yet allowed for disagreement. Determining the logistics of how to conduct the research was complicated and took much time; Patricia, Penny Poplin Gosetti, and the Xavier rector made most of the logistical decisions.

We worked most actively with Xavier in 1992–1993 and 1993–1994, using Grove and St. Elizabeth's as companion comparisons. Xavier became our primary focus for several reasons: (1) it remained all-male during the first year of research, whereas Grove had already begun the four-year process of admitting boys to the freshman class; (2) the majority of Xavier teachers were willing to participate actively in the research and were eager to gain assistance during the final transition years; and (3) the male principal and male rector were curious, open, helpful and sincerely wished to create an environment for girls that was as good as it was for boys. We believed their curiosity and support were essential to carrying out the kind of research we wanted to do.

Research Tasks

We sought to answer our research questions using both qualitative and quantitative methods. Sources for data came from six general research foci that included: (a) school policy and administration, (b) curriculum, (c) pedagogy, (d) student outcomes, (e) school culture, and (f) faculty action research. Table 1.1 summarizes the data we derived from the following research tasks:

1   interviewing each member of the Xavier faculty, analyzing and categorizing the data, and presenting the data to the faculty in a large meeting;
2   meeting with the research steering committee composed of administrators, teachers, and members of the research team;
3   observing classrooms, analyzing data, and meeting with the teachers involved;
4   recording and analyzing archival materials;
5   interviewing relevant groups such as trustees;
6   conducting student focus groups;
7   holding follow-up focus groups with faculty; and

Table 1.1 *Summary of Data Collection Activities*

Types of Data	School Year, 1992–1993	School Year, 1993–1994
I Individual Interviews:		
Teachers	X, SE	X, SE
Administrators	X, SE	S, SE
Staff	X	S
Board members	X	
Students:		
Females	X, SE	X, SE
Males	X	
II Surveys:		
Teachers		X
Administrators		X
Staff		X
Students:		
Female		X
Male	X	X
III Focus Groups:		
Teachers and Staff		X
Students:		
Female	X, SE, G	X, SE, G
Male		X
IV Classroom/School Studies:		
Observations	X, SE, G	X, SE, G
Sadker Instrument	X, SE, G	X, SE, G
V Archival Data:		
Historical documents	X, SE, G	
School calendars	X, SE, G	
Course offerings	X, SE, G	
Enrollment information	X, SE, G	
Textbook analysis	X, SE, G	
Faculty professional experience	X	
Mission statements	X, SE, G	

Notes:
X Xavier Prep
SE St. Elizabeth's Academy
G Grove Catholic High

8   collecting and analyzing data on mathematics test scores and student performance, curricula and instructional practices.

Conceptual Foundations

As we began our research tasks, we intended to understand better the experiences of young men and young women in single-sex and coeducational school and classroom environments. With time, however, our study became far more complex and we gradually changed our focus to address the issues and themes that began to emerge from the data. We came to understand the emerging data through perspectives drawn from the literature on feminist methodologies, Catholic education, single-sex education and coeducation, gender consciousness and privilege.

A Feminist Research Perspective

The qualitative and quantitative methods described in the research tasks above are frequently used by researchers in the social sciences. The framework and perspective from which we approached the methods, however, reflected a feminist stance; a view that constantly challenged us to examine the schools and their contexts critically from the standpoint of being female. Although we did not begin the study with the intention to "do" feminist research, we recognized that we were a group of researchers who shared a distinct concern about young women's experience in high school. And we shared feminist perspectives on research; we believed in using women's experiences as a basis for our analysis (Harding, 1987) and putting the social construction of gender at the center of our inquiry (Lather, 1991). We also valued using personal reflection to uncover embedded assumptions about gender relations, and in participating in collaborative scholarship (Fonow and Cook, 1991).

Those feminist perspectives focused us on embedded ideas of gender by identifying what Smith (1987) calls "fault lines," those points of rupture that exist between what traditional knowledge tells women they experience and what women actually experience in their everyday lives. Much of our research entailed listening to female voices speak of their experience and interpreting that data through a feminist lens. While our research focus eventually developed into trying to understand gender consciousness and the effects of privilege in constructing gender in schools, we never lost sight of our original intention – to use the opportunity provided by three Catholic high schools to learn about gender and the female experience in single-sex and coeducational schools.

The Catholic Context

Catholic schooling has a long and rich history in the United States; it constitutes the largest subset of private and independent schools. Built up from
colonial times it has no other parallel in the world; the American Catholic
System is distinctively American (Bryk et al., 1993). With a long-standing
commitment to serving the educational needs of all children regardless of
socioeconomic status, its formation was closely aligned with the mission to
provide a common school for the nation (NCEA, 1985). Catholic schools
increasingly serve diverse student populations, and in the last twenty years,
they have maintained a stable presence in many poor, ethnic minority, and
urban neighborhoods. Catholic schools are committed to traditional
academic programs including the teaching of religion and values (Buetow,
1988). In 1993–1994, Catholic schools enrolled approximately 5.3 percent of
the total U.S. student body in grades 3–12 (McArthur, 1995).

Parents enroll their children in Catholic schools for two reasons: they
perceive that their children will have a better academic experience than in
the public schools, and will have the opportunity for religious or moral
training (Bryk et al., 1993). Evidently parents whose children are in Catholic
schools are pleased with their choice; 90 percent of those parents report
positive perceptions of the school, curriculum, and the faculty (McArthur,
1995). Not surprisingly, parents of children in all forms of private schools
are satisfied with their children's education; if they were not pleased, they
would remove their child.

In general, students in Catholic schools are more well off financially than
their counterparts in public schools, with family incomes averaging $34,000
as compared to $28,000 for those in public schools. Only 16 percent of chil-
dren in Catholic schools come from single-parent families as compared to
28 percent in public schools. Compared to children in public schools, more
children in Catholic schools have parents with higher educational levels, live
in households that receive a daily newspaper, and have designated places in
the household to study (Bryk et al., 1993, p. 70).

Some argue that the success of Catholic school students, who consistently
demonstrate higher levels of academic achievement than do public school
students, occurs because Catholic schools select their clients (Bryk et al.,
1993; Cibulka et al., 1982; Coleman and Hoffer, 1987). The "selectivity
hypothesis" posits that family background is the important variable in
Catholic students' achievement. To test this hypothesis, one would have to
compare achievement of students with similar family backgrounds in public
schools. However, we offer an argument of Bryk et al. (1993) that changes
the locus of responsibility from the family to the school. They say:

> From our perspective the continued reliance on the selectivity hypo-
> thesis as an explanation for Catholic school effects is part of a larger
> world view in which individuals are seen as primary and the operations

of institutions as simply an aggregate manifestation of individuals pursuing their self interest. In contrast, our results indicate that *teachers and administrators can organize their work in different ways, can create more engaging environments, and, as a result, can have a very different effect on students* (emphasis ours).

(p. 294)

Bryk et al. (1993) posit that three factors about school organizations create successful Catholic high schools: (1) Most students are channeled into a common or core set of academic courses that lead to the integration of school life for students and administration; (2) A "communal organization" exists that offers a variety of activities that promote interaction among students and adults; and (3) Students and faculty share a common set of beliefs about student learning, student conduct, and future goals and values. Those shared beliefs contribute to the inspirational ideology, which creates a moral authority and a strong sense of purpose at the school (Bryk et al., 1993).

In addition to sharing common values and visions at successful Catholic high schools, students, parents, and faculty have made a deliberate choice to participate. Catholic schools can remove students who do not fit into the prevailing culture; not only is the community voluntary, it is dependent on institutional selection. Erving Goffman (1959) pointed out some years ago that public schools have no say in the selection of their clientele, in this way public schools are like prisons and mental hospitals; they must take whoever comes to the door. What we may learn from these settings, however, is how to create public school organizations that include those factors that influence students such as building community, developing common purpose, and creating school organizations with a strong moral base.[1] Effective public schools exist that demonstrate those criteria across the social class scale (Edmonds, 1979; Leithwood et al., 1992).

Catholic Schools and Sex Segregation

In the United States, secondary education historically was for boys. Girls were "smuggled" into public high schools in the mid-nineteenth century and they stayed, willingly paying the tuition required by early schools. They compliantly followed the designated curriculum and they were successful students (Tyack and Hansot, 1990).[2] While the public schools became co-educational in the mid-nineteenth century, most Catholic schools remained single-sex into the mid-twentieth century.

By 1983, about 46 percent of Catholic high schools were single-sex; about 21 percent were male-only schools and about 25 percent were female-only schools. In the ensuing decade the male-only schools were reduced to 18 percent, whereas the number of female-only schools remained the same

15

(Bryk et al., 1993). At the same time, the percentage of non-white pupils enrolled in Catholic schools increased from 16.3 percent in 1982 to 23.2 percent in 1992 and the percentage of non-Catholics increased in that period as well. Moreover, the teaching staffs within Catholic secondary schools continued to undergo significant change with the number of lay teachers growing to approximately 84 percent of staff (Brigham, 1993 as cited in LePore and Warren, 1997).

Catholic schools at all grade levels are becoming more heterogeneous in all respects. High schools have bent to the common argument that coeducation provides a more natural social environment to prepare adolescents to take their place in society than does single-sex schooling, thus few single-sex Catholic high schools are left in the United States, and those that are left may provide unique contexts for studying issues related to gender and education.

Single-sex and Coeducation: Confronting Conflicting Research

For the first time in the United States in about a century, a rising interest in single-sex and coeducation at the federal policy level is occurring. Although a general consensus exists that coeducation does not hurt males' academic achievement and that the presence of girls can be a quieting and civilizing effect on adolescent males (Dale, 1969, 1971, 1974),[3] the literature on single-sex and coeducational schooling is conflicting and controversial, especially about females' experiences. Some data suggest female academic achievement and self-esteem may be higher in single-sex school organizations (Shmurak, 1998; Streitmatter, 1998), but LePore and Warren's findings (1997) of female and male achievement at the 10th grade levels indicate no discernible positive effect of single-sex or coeducation on academic performance or measures of self-esteem. Recent research on the merits of single-sex or coeducation for both males and females calls into question the findings of studies conducted in the 1970s and 1980s; we cannot assume that one environment is *categorically* better for one group of students over another (see Chapter 5, this volume for another example of this discussion).

The debate about single-sex and coeducational schooling has shifted away from the sex comparisons of male and female achievement and self-esteem to better understand the nature of the experiences of females and males within particular contexts. Recent research on academic achievement, identity formation, and self-esteem is worth considering, however, because it points to the complexity of the issues and the need for studies that explore the school context in more depth. What is increasingly apparent is that identity and self-esteem are complex, multifaceted constructs, and different environments may cultivate and support different aspects of those constructs (Proweller, 1998; Shmurak, 1998). Three studies, in particular, raise questions about previous research findings that suggested female academic achievement and self-esteem may be higher in single-sex schools than in coeducational schools.

Marsh et al. (1988) studied two public, single-sex high schools serving the same neighborhood in a metropolitan area of Australia that were reorganized to form two coeducational high schools. Using two measures of self-esteem to capture multidimensional facets of this construct, they studied the effects of the transition to coeducation for all students. Both boys and girls experienced a clear increase in multidimensional self-concepts from the pre-transition to the post-transition, despite a small decrease in self-concepts for students attending coed classes during the transition. Sex differences in specific areas of self-concept – those favoring boys and those favoring girls – were unaffected by the transition. Analysis of achievement scores across the four years of the study using state tests indicated there were substantial differences between girls' and boys' performance in mathematics and English achievement – girls performed substantially better than boys in English and relatively poorer in mathematics – however, the sizes of those differences were unaffected by the transition. In terms of the transition effect, this study confirmed earlier studies (Dale, 1969, 1971, 1974) that showed a significant improvement for girls' and boys' self-concept and little influence on academic achievement.

LePore and Warren (1997) used data from the National Educational Longitudinal Study of 1988 to examine whether differences existed between single-sex and coeducational Catholic secondary school students in academic and social psychological outcomes and whether those differences favored young women in single-sex schools. They found that boys in single-sex schools have higher achievement test scores in grades 8, 10, and 12 than boys in coeducational schools, but they do not appear to *learn* more, that is, across the high school years, boys in single-sex schools do not increase their test scores any more than boys in coeducational schools. For girls, however, they could not conclude that single-sex Catholic schools are more advantageous academic settings than coeducational settings.

LePore and Warren's research conflicts with the "High School and Beyond" studies of Lee and Bryk (1986) and other research (Marsh et al., 1989; Willis and Kenway, 1986) that asserted single-sex Catholic secondary schools are more effective than coeducational Catholic secondary schools for both boys and girls in terms of achievement – particularly in traditionally gender stereotyped areas such as reading, writing, science, and math.

The notion that girls will perform better in liberal arts subjects, whereas boys typically will perform better in math and science, has been challenged in a four-year study conducted by researchers from Educational Testing Service (Willingham and Cole, 1997). They found that gender gaps in the United States are not nearly as large or as pervasive as one might think. Evidence exists that the gaps between boys and girls that were visible in 1960 have narrowed considerably in math and science, with data from 1990 showing no male advantage in either subject. But when they broke down math into its component subject areas, they found females did slightly better on some subskills and males did better on others; the same held true for language arts. Another major finding was that although the gaps across subject areas were minimal at the 4th grade level, gender differences grew by the time students reach the 12th grade depending on the subject area; for example, girls' advantage in writing grew substantially between 4th and 8th grade, whereas boys' advantage in natural science did not occur until some-'time between 8th and 12th grade.

Those subtle differences in outcomes and gaps in performance periods indicate that the factors relative to achievement, self-esteem, and gender are more complex than traditional methods of understanding can allow. Researchers now emphasize the need to understand how individual unique-ness impacts gender. They recognize that achievement test scores do not convey wholly what is learned in school. Similarly, the typical constructs for understanding self-esteem may not adequately tap into the hidden curriculum of schools and the implicit assumptions conveyed through school culture and subcultures. Indeed, educators call for the need to under-stand how and in what ways gender discrimination exists in so far that it is a more subtle and complex problem than implied by past research. LePore and Warren (1997) point out that the limited research indicates that sexism occurs in all school sectors regardless of gender composition, but that its complexion and contour will not be understood until we have more case studies of school life in context.

Developing the Concept of Gender Consciousness

An awareness of sex bias and discrimination among teachers and students is an important change in schools and society that resulted from the 1972 Title IX reforms. LePore and Warren (1997) point out, however, that "gender discrimination is a far more subtle and complex problem than is implied by past research. ... Incidences of sexism occur in all school sectors regardless of gender composition" (p. 506). Shmurak (1998) and Lee (1997) would agree. Shmurak, in her study of adolescent girls in single-sex and coeduca-tional environments, found different *types* of sexist practices at different types of schools: whereas females were affirmed in all-female environments, in coeducational environments they experienced blatant sex discrimination.

Today most educators agree that schools should eliminate inequitable practices for females and males. Title IX has provided a legal remedy to provide the same opportunities for females as for males. However, while educators are aware of the need to eliminate sex bias and sexist practices, they are not always aware of the sexism and inequality embedded in many school policies and practices and in some teacher behaviors. The awareness of embedded sexism and inequality in our schools is a level of consciousness about gender that moves us further than simply eliminating the sex bias or discrimination addressed in Title IX. Developing consciousness about gender and privilege is a *process*, not an achieved state. The concept of *gender consciousness* begins with acceptance of equality of the sexes; where schools are:

> providing the same access and treatment to female and male learners either "within the same context" or possibly in a separate (sex segregated) but equal context ... [or] providing differential access and treatment to female and male learners based on their [individual] needs, their [individual] merit, or their [individual] ends and merit combined.
>
> (Klein, Russo, Campbell, and Harvey as cited in Klein and Ortman, 1994, p. 13)

Gender consciousness is also relative; it is a matter of degree regarding sex and gender equity. There are differences among practices associated with unexamined, sex-equitable, gender-aware, and critical transformative thoughts and behaviors when considering school climate, culture, and policies, as well as classroom instruction and curricular materials. Practices associated with *unexamined thoughts and behaviors* typically are recognized in traditionally stereotypical expectations and processes that reinforce narrow definitions of behaviors based on normative characteristics ascribed to the different sexes. *Sex-equity* practices focus on the *equal* treatment of males and females; they emphasize the elimination of common and overt stereotypes in language usage, classroom management practices, teaching materials, and so on, and attempt to rectify imbalances based on sex.[4] *Gender-awareness* practices result from recognizing the deeply embedded cultural meanings of being male and female and questioning the gendered assumptions that guide the organizational setting, classroom life, and teaching and learning practices. Sex-equity and gender-awareness practices grow out of a consciousness about working for sex and gender equity, but each reflects a different degree of understanding, response, and willingness to change the conditions.[5] *Critical transformative* practices, on the other hand, reflect a central understanding of the role privilege plays in maintaining gender inequities, and work toward recognizing and encouraging multiple perspectives in ways that privilege no one.

The Role of Privilege

Privilege is a concept tied to images of status and wealth. As seen from its traditional roots in European nobility and the aristocracy, privilege is an idea that belies the American ideals of "equal rights for all, special privileges for none" (Jefferson as cited in George, 1906, p. 17). Defined in those terms, privilege is easy to identify, but not often claimed by any but the wealthy

(Gosetti, 1995). Researchers suggest, however, that privilege has dimensions that are hidden by traditional economic definitions. Peggy McIntosh (1988), for instance, defines privilege as unearned and frequently taken-for-granted advantages accrued purely through one's birth into a certain group. She suggests that privilege exists, unseen, within our social systems. As such, it gives people choices, opportunities, dominance and permission to control members of less privileged groups (Bohmer and Briggs, 1991) while making those power relationships appear as natural.

Many authors point out the privileges that are conferred through visible group affiliations based on skin color and sex (Angus, 1993; Bohmer and Briggs, 1991; McIntosh, 1988; Sleeter, 1993). For example, social privileges of sex exist that grant cultural, professional, and personal status to men in ways that dominate and marginalize women. People also experience privilege based on the type of education they receive (Hilliard, 1988), and the single-sex or coeducational settings in which they receive their education (Riordan, 1990; Sadker and Sadker, 1994). Some group affiliations, such as religion (e.g., Catholics), are less visible but are tied to an attribute that is valued and, therefore, privileged over other attributes. Examples of such groups are those that have the power to create and name knowledge (Fowlkes, 1992; Tirrell, 1993), to control knowledge distribution (Jansen, 1989), and to define the use of language (Lewis and Simon, 1986).

As individuals become more conscious of gender, they may begin to see privilege as the special advantages a person has simply by being a member of a particular group. Our educational systems, however, provide barriers to recognizing privilege by teaching members of the dominant cultural group that their lives are "morally neutral, normative, average, and also ideal" (McIntosh, 1988, p. 3). These systems, traditionally, have not helped members of dominant groups to see themselves as privileged and unfairly advantaged. Many who enjoy the privileges of a system that perpetuates their privileged status are not even aware that the system exists.

Gender Consciousness, Privilege, and Culture

The changes brought about in three Catholic high schools by Xavier's decision to become coeducational provided us the opportunity to examine the consciousness of school cultures where members were questioning "the way it is" about sex, gender, single-sex education, and coeducation. They were unique settings for uncovering cultural assumptions, intentions, and behavior. The dissonance created by change and transition opened the door for educators and students to become aware of the assumptions in their culture. In times of change, when "business as usual" is interrupted participants may see more easily into their organizations' hidden dimensions of privilege. The knowledge provided by the conceptual foundations described above helped us examine whether privilege and constructions of knowledge about gender greatly influenced the cultural assumptions and consciousness of these schools.

Notes

1 Many educational texts make the same argument that community and school organizations can be created to maximize student achievement. See, for instance, Schmuck and Schmuck, 1996.

2 This is an excellent history of coeducation in the United States. We do, however, take issue with Tyack and Hansot that schools are the most "gender neutral" institutions in society. This theme is addressed in a review of their work by Edson and Schmuck, 1992.

3 These three volumes are perhaps the most comprehensive studies. They are about British schools that had a long tradition of single-sex schooling that changed toward coeducation about the 1960s.

4 The policy debates in the 1970s and 1980s on whether males and females were more alike than different dramatically influenced the shaping of Title IX legislation and the concept of sex equity. Eleanor Maccoby and Carolyn Jacklin (1974), in their meta-analysis of sex difference in psychological studies, asserted females and males were more alike than different. They argued that institutions determined the degree to which females and males were different, asserting that societies have the option of minimizing, rather than maximizing sex differences.

5 By the 1980s, feminist academics began paying attention to the special qualities of being female, rather than focusing on how females were like males (see, for example, Belenky et al., 1986; Gilligan, 1982; Miller, 1976, 1986). These scholars addressed psychological research conducted on males, the findings of which were held to be universally true for all human beings; these scholars found when women were the subjects for study they did not fit the same developmental and psychological patterns as males; women were essentially different from males, but the essential differences were not necessarily attributed to biology; they probably were learned. The significance of this contribution was to shift the unquestioned, positive status and value implied in the masculine construct and generalize to the value of other kinds of difference, particularly those qualities traditionally ascribed to females and to the construction of the feminine. These researchers made the nature vs. nurture debate about sex differences even more complex, and contributed to the development of the concept of gender as a social construction. The research on differences between females and males in brain functions, hormonal patterns, and evolutionary biology continues to grow. But significant disagreements continue in terms of the meanings of those differences.

2 Faculty Constructions of Gender at Xavier Preparatory High School

Literature on sex equity and school reform during the last two decades clearly shows that successful school change occurs with an aggressive and conscious commitment to it on the part of staff members. According to the research, difficulties that staff members have in providing equal educational opportunities to all students and in coping with the complexities of change include: their overt communication and covert meanings, their articulated beliefs and unstated assumptions, and how their expectations are communicated and realized (Lockheed and Hall, 1976; Sadker et al., 1991; Tetreault, 1986; Tetreault and Schmuck, 1985). We believed like other researchers what teachers thought about gender and what they expected would happen when young women entered their classroom and their school represented critical factors in how the change would be implemented (Clark and Peterson, 1986; Cuban, 1988; Doyle and Ponder, 1977; Fullan, 1991; Richardson et al., 1991). Acknowledging the difficulties and subtleties of the challenges the faculty and students faced, we sought to understand how the faculty framed issues of fairness and sex equity in the post-Title IX era.

In this chapter, we describe what Xavier teachers, administrators, and classified members anticipated about issues of gender and equity as their school changed from all-male to coeducational. How would faculty members perceive female students after thirty-two years of being an all-male school? How would they view the entering females? What would be their expectations? How would these expectations influence what happened in the classroom? In the school? Would teachers think change was needed to accommodate females? If so, what changes would be needed? In pedagogy? The curriculum? The classroom? The school?

Gathering Data About Faculty Construction of Gender

At the outset, our research team, committed to participatory action research (Hollingsworth, 1994; Schmuck, 1997), hoped to help the Xavier faculty reflect on their own staff development activities and better accommodate the newly entering females by fostering a learning community with high consciousness about gender. We eschewed the role of researcher as outsider

22

and controller of the data, expecting to share information in a formative way for faculty to use. Our data collection and analysis focused on three sources:

1   structured interviews with the entire staff – teachers, support staff, and administration – in the Spring prior to the move to coeducation;
2   small-group discussions with faculty and administrators in the winter of the first year of coeducation; and
3   written surveys obtained from administrators and returning and new faculty in the spring of the first year of coeducation.

Structured Interviews

Researchers interviewed seventy-two people at Xavier over a two-week period in the winter prior to coeducation (see Table 2.1). The interviewees included all teachers, administrators, support staff, and some trustees at Xavier High School. A planning committee composed of our research team, the principal and rector from Xavier, the principal of St. Elizabeth's, and two teacher representatives from Xavier developed the interview schedule. Research team members conducted fifty-minute individual interviews focused on the anticipated change to coeducation. (See Appendix A for the complete interview protocol.) We recorded and transcribed each interview.

We heard from administrators and teachers that the interviews themselves were having a positive, healing effect on the previously divided faculty. A range of attitudes from rejection to acceptance of coeducation had developed during the five years of planning. The interviews made clear to everyone, whether they agreed with the decision to become coeducational or not, that young women would enter Xavier the next fall. Prior to the structured interviews the faculty had addressed sex-biased language and differences in male–female conversation, using Deborah Tannen's (1990) book, *You Just Don't Understand*, as the focus of their work. Although the interviews were voluntary, no one refused to be interviewed. Many faculty and staff began their interviews by saying they had looked forward to them because they had heard from previous interviewees that the interviews promoted personal reflection facilitated by a respectful listener. With a major change at Xavier on the horizon, they valued the importance of open talk. Every staff member, teacher, and administrator, whether they had been for or against coeducation, wanted to provide an excellent education to the young men and young women at Xavier. We saw no evidence of anyone, regardless of their beliefs about coeducation, wanting to sabotage efforts to provide an exemplary education to all students.

Still, mixed opinions remained on the Xavier faculty about the advisability of becoming coeducational even after five years of discussion and preparation. Some faculty opposed coeducation, fervently believing that

23

Table 2.1 Demographics of Teacher Interview Participants at Xavier During the Transition to Coeducation

Category	Totals ($n = 59$)
Male	40
Female	19
Religious	5
Lay	54
Catholic	39
Non-Catholic	20
Age:	
20–30	7
31–40	13
41–50	18
51–60	7
61+	3
Missing cases	11
Years taught/worked at Xavier:	
0–2	18
3–5	13
6+	20
Missing cases	8
Assignment:	
Teacher	47
Staff	12
Taught Previously in Coed. Setting	31
Missing cases	11

single-sex education better served the interests of young men and their Catholic heritage. Conversely, others believed that it was time for Xavier to "enter the 20th century" since males and females increasingly work side by side in most walks of life.

We deliberately designed the interview protocol to help Xavier faculty members better understand their collective beliefs about the value of co-education and what changes would or would not be necessary in instruction, curriculum, and student life. At the time of the interviews faculty consciousness about gender was high; we expected to see faculty express their most developed consciousness about gender and sex equity and fairness.

Using methods derived from grounded theory, we divided the data into categories, matching each response to the appropriate category and coding it accordingly (Strauss and Corbin, 1994). Four themes emerged from the interviews about areas the faculty emphasized:

1   the community
2   educational philosophy and the curriculum
3   pedagogy and classroom relationships
4   extra-curricular activities

In some areas faculty members expected to make or to see change occur while in others they expected no changes. We used the four categories to develop a series of questions that we used with student focus groups during the first year of coeducation and to organize our thinking about the various kinds of data gathered.

When we shared some of our initial impressions with the planning team (including the Xavier administrators) we began to realize for the first time that our goals as the research team might not match the goals of our Xavier colleagues. We included in the feedback our observation that Xavier faculty members had not addressed issues of what was good for females during the interviews – only what was good for males. We describe this incident elsewhere (in Chapter 6) as noting "silences" – recognizing those topics or ideas that were markedly absent in the faculty responses to interview questions. Xavier committee members disagreed that silences were data. In the spring, during the final months of Xavier's existence as an all-male school, we provided feedback about our data to the entire faculty, this time excluding any discussion of "silences." Unfortunately, the shortness of the meeting did not permit time for dialogue between the faculty and our research team; we learned afterward that many faculty viewed positively our approach to presenting what we learned about their beliefs and thinking. They felt neither threatened nor challenged.

Small-Group Discussions

During the first year of coeducation we held monthly one-hour group discussions with the entire faculty and staff, including newcomers, drawing upon the themes gleaned from initial individual interviews. Each group had between four and ten participants. We led three different kinds of small-group discussions: (1) structured teacher groups, including newcomers; (2) structured administrator groups; and (3) six open-forum sessions for faculty and administrators. The open forum primarily attracted the few teachers who expressed concerns and doubts about how smoothly everything was going.

Written Surveys

In the spring of the transition year to coeducation, we administered a follow-up written survey asking faculty members to describe surprises in the key themes they identified the year before: school culture, student interactions, curriculum, instruction, and teaching. Thirty-seven returning teachers and administrators, and twelve new teachers and administrators completed written follow-up surveys. (The teacher questionnaire is included as Appendix B.)

Teachers' Gender Consciousness

Developing consciousness about gender is a learning process; teachers are at different stages of thinking about the influences of sex for themselves and their students. There is a continuum of development of gender consciousness. Teachers' expectations about sex influence their evaluation of students and their behaviors toward them (Finn, 1980; Haller, 1985). Even in an all-male and all-Caucasian school, teachers' concepts about sex influence their classroom and school practices. Along with those teachers' behaviors, school-wide policies and practices also influence students' thinking about themselves. For instance, in many schools educators differ in their disciplinary practices for young women and young men; the curriculum communicates, either overtly or covertly, what the school and community values; and student peer expectations also communicate powerful messages about gender.

In this section, we introduce the importance of teachers' thinking about gender as a key feature in school culture and student learning. We describe different amounts of gender consciousness that we unearthed as we analyzed data from individual and small-group interviews and as we observed teacher practices which were based on thinking about gender. We refer to these different degrees of thinking about gender as "gender consciousness." Gender consciousness refers to a person's readiness to recognize how sex differences and privilege are deeply embedded in the assumptions, expectations, practices, and manifestations of the society. Such a recognition is necessary to authentically teach students to openly examine and respond to issues of unearned privilege in order to achieve equity.

A Continuum of Gender Consciousness and Privilege

Figure 2.1 characterizes four degrees of difference along a continuum from no consciousness about gender to a strong belief in critical transformation. It is important to recognize that while individuals or institutions might move over time from lesser toward greater gender consciousness, their typical growth pattern is uneven and complex. In this study, we witnessed the highly context-bound nature of individual beliefs and behaviors, and institutional policies and procedures. Movement toward greater gender consciousness did not occur as a simple linear progression. In Chapter 7, we describe how the social context, the school culture, the faculty beliefs about gender, and the students' perceptions interact to create complex, context-embedded, and uncertain terrain about gender and privilege. The continuum is described here only briefly and presented in more detail in Chapter 7.

Figure 2.1   *Continuum of Gender Consciousness and Privilege*

Position 0. Unexamined Thoughts and Behaviors
Position 1. Sex Equity
Position 2. Gender Awareness
Position 3. Critical Transformation

Position 0: Unexamined Thoughts and Behaviors

Individuals operating at this point on the continuum unquestioningly accept social assumptions and stereotypes for females and males on the basis of sex. They may deny bias and discrimination has occurred for them or for others. Such individuals believe treating people the same is treating them equitably.

Schools intentionally or unintentionally implement different standards, policies, and behavioral consequences for females and males.

Position 1: Sex Equity

Individuals recognize females and males are treated differently because of their sex; they make some corrective actions for same treatment. They do not question whether equal treatment leads to equal outcomes.

Schools change standards and policies that differentiate on account of sex and provide deliberate compensatory opportunities to redress past inequities on account of sex.

Position 2: Gender Awareness

Individuals recognize same treatment is not always equitable and the cultural meanings of being female or male are deeply embedded in everyone's thinking and behavior; the concept of "sex" changes to the concept of "gender."

Schools question the assumptions guiding teaching and learning, curricular choices, and extra-curricular activities. The staff looks more deeply into how gender is expressed and revealed in teaching, classroom group processes, and school organizational functioning.

Position 3: Critical Transformation

Individuals recognize the unspoken assumptions of social privilege, which is determined by valued position in the society. They see that one's sex, social class, and race enable some individuals to have privilege and access to societal rewards, while others do not have the same privilege or access to rewards.

Schools help students question unearned privilege and social dominance in the community and society; the curricula move toward understanding multiple perspectives on reality and encourage students to question critically interpretations of world events. Schools at Position 3 routinely use a critical-theory perspective as an integral part of the curriculum.

Xavier Teachers' Constructions of Gender

Our individual and group interviews with Xavier teachers revealed that the overwhelming majority of teachers saw themselves at Position 1, the sex equity level of consciousness. They saw a need to eliminate sex bias in their classrooms, the school, and the society, but they did not see a need to change their teaching methods or curriculum when young women entered their classrooms. They believed they were already doing what was good for students in general and that their mission to create community leaders committed to serve God and their fellow human beings was morally correct. They believed that what was good for males in single-sex Xavier would also be equally good for males and females in coeducational Xavier.

Xavier did anticipate providing certain support for females beyond new lavatories and locker rooms. Counselors, for instance, had never dealt with issues of maternity (they had not dealt with paternity issues either), and sexual behavior took on new meaning for rules of conduct. School planning in preparation for the coeducation transition included attention to such obvious differential needs of females, but anticipated minimal changes otherwise. For example, instructional innovations aimed at specifically meeting the needs of females were not considered on an institution-wide basis. Such strategies were left to individual teachers, if they were considered at all.

In general, Xavier teachers wanted to enact objective standards to guard against preferential or differing treatment on the basis of sex. They wanted to ensure sex equity in order to avoid sex bias and discrimination. In the teaching of their classes, assigning activities, and setting behavioral expectations, teachers sought to implement same practices for females and males; they wanted to equalize male and female access by offering the same resources in talk, teacher attention, assignments, and expectations. For instance, Charlene Wilson, the high school English teacher at Xavier, used the same curriculum in her coeducational classroom that she had used in her all-male classroom. When some young women objected to the absence of female authors or protagonists in all their reading, Mrs. Wilson[1] understood she had to change the curriculum to provide more equal representation of access to both male and female voices in literature. We believe that in doing so she was moving to a different level of gender consciousness. Most of her colleagues did not, however, make such changes, at least not during the first years of coeducation.

Xavier Preparatory's goal for the transition was to implement sex equity in a coeducational school. Three components were essential to achieving the desired coeducational school. First, maintaining a loving and just community, a resounding theme in our initial interviews, remained at the center of this mission. Second, the faculty was deeply committed to the curriculum established by Ignatius Loyola in the sixteenth century. Third, the faculty wanted to eliminate sex biases in their classrooms and their school. In the following sections we will describe each of these themes in detail.

A Community of Shared Commitments

Xavier faculty members expressed strong beliefs in the value of community. They had developed an intentional community to create strong leaders; their mission had been to graduate servant leaders "who are men for others." They wanted for young women the same education that they had successfully provided for young men, to graduate servant leaders "who are men and women for others."

Xavier faculty and staff were strongly committed to the school community; they chose to teach and work at Xavier and by and large felt pleased with their choice. They expressed a sincere hope that the change to coeducation not disturb the meaning and practice of community life at Xavier. Although they did not believe that the presence of young women would disturb the community, they were quite concerned about the increased size of the school as a result of coeducation.

The influence of size

Enrollment predictions projected an increase in size of 30 percent in the first year of coeducation, from 600 to 860 students, rising to 1,000 students by the third year; the number of new teachers would also increase. For many faculty and staff, the presence of young women *per se* had less to do with the potential loss of special male bonding than the effect of increased numbers on the greatly valued community where they knew each student personally, and where faculty interacted daily with each other. As expected, the move to coeducation not only brought young women into Xavier classrooms, but also produced crowded conditions for students and teachers, particularly in the hallways and cafeteria. Many teachers spoke of having less contact outside of class with students and colleagues. A single shared lunch time, for example, became two lunch periods, splitting up students and faculty, affecting friends and relationships. For the most part, however, staff and faculty expressed surprise at how smoothly the transition had occurred.

Changes in "the burping, farting culture"

Although they expected the all-male tradition would change somewhat, most staff and faculty wanted to maintain school traditions. Many did express hope that certain negative behaviors would change; that young women might positively affect what one teacher called "the burping, farting culture" of an all-male school. The staff hoped the presence of females would have a "softening effect"; that young women would have a "civilizing," "kinder, gentler" effect on the male energy that historically characterized daily life at Xavier Preparatory prior to coeducation – a common phenomenon in all-male high schools.

The real world of females and males

Most staff hoped the influence of coeducation would normalize the atmosphere at Xavier, bringing to it a "real-world" dimension of men and women learning and working together. A small number of teachers expressed concern about the potential loss of the caring and nurturing outlets available to the young men. They feared, as did many of the young men, that the easy male-to-male relationships would change with the presence of young women.

Changing a sexist culture

Nearly 25 percent of the staff worried that young women would feel unwanted; and some questioned whether young women could ever become truly integrated. A minority of women faculty hoped that coeducation would change the behavior and attitudes of students and teachers they labeled as sexist.

Ignatian Educational Philosophy and Curriculum

The Xavier faculty was committed to the educational principles established by Ignatius Loyola in the first part of the sixteenth century. Teaching at

Xavier means that one adheres to Ignatian philosophy and helps continue to build a strong community. Sixty-four percent of the staff pointed to their belief in the Ignatian philosophy which defined their own educational philosophy: "Everyone can learn, students are accountable for their own learning, and high standards develop leaders." Faculty responses reflected the school's mission – to "foster the harmonious development of the adolescent's gifts: spiritual, religious, intellectual, physical, emotional, aesthetic." Most Xavier educators, lay or religious, administrator or teacher, believe they are good teachers and that their colleagues are good teachers. They love their work. They believe Xavier is a special place for students and for adults.

We believe that some of those faculty expectations affected their perceptions about what occurred in the school and classrooms during the first year of coeducation. Most faculty members shared the view that the traditional philosophy, curriculum, and goals were essentially good for everyone. Curriculum was a given, set in the classic, Western tradition in which students learn and master content for college admission. The teachers' goal was to guard against sex bias and treat females as they had treated males. Changes would occur only when sex bias was obvious.

Though most teachers expressed commitment to the Ignatian philosophy, they differed in their interpretations of that philosophy and in where they placed themselves on a philosophical continuum. Some teachers saw themselves as solidly within the conservative academic tradition; students were accountable to learn the material assigned, listen to lectures, and do well on tests. Students did not need "coddling." These conservative teachers tended to question the decision about whether coeducation was a good idea and they saw little need to change their pedagogy or curriculum. Teachers on the more progressive end of the philosophical continuum saw themselves as more student-centered; they believed curriculum should focus on current social relevance. These more liberal teachers said, "curriculum ought to address issues that students face, such as abortion," and "teachers have a responsibility to relate the content to students' personal lives and develop independent, critical thinkers"; they believed in a teacher's obligation to reach students, drawing upon a key aspect of Ignatian pedagogy, to help the student be the best she or he can be, developing personal talents as far as possible.

While everyone agreed that students were "accountable for their own learning," some of the more progressive teachers believed that certain of the self-proclaimed traditional, highly directive teachers were using student accountability as a smoke screen for not being more interactive and engaged with students. Some predicted that these more traditional teachers would have difficulties with female students because they already had problems with male students. They believed teachers who lectured most of the time, did not engage in dialogue with students, and were not willing to let students work with one another, used the notion of accountability as an excuse for not modernizing their teaching strategies.

The majority of Xavier teachers, about 70 percent, believed the Ignatian pedagogical tradition was being redefined from traditional to progressive and they were the bearers of this new more student-oriented order. These teachers described a commitment to educate the whole person – including feelings and attitudes, regard for diversity in a changing world and more student-focused and student-centered classrooms.

Pedagogy and Classroom Relationships

We asked faculty members whether they would need to change their teaching methods with the presence of young women in their classrooms. Eliminating sex bias was the objective for most of the faculty and administration as they prepared for young women to enter Xavier. They sought to build an environment of sex equity; they believed treating female and male students alike would take care of any inequalities. Generally speaking, they were determined not to show favoritism, believed they were not sex-biased, and planned to continue their same methods of teaching, which they believed would be just as successful with young women as it had been with young men.

Faculty members knew that sexual harassment would no longer be an abstraction, and that the Xavier community would have to rethink the use of previously unquestioned male symbols such as the school mascot, "Nate the Knight." We uncovered three topics of teachers' response about what they believed should change in their classroom with the entrance of young women: (1) language, (2) discipline and classroom management, and (3) patterns of classroom interaction.

Language: the litmus test of sex bias

Over the five years of planning for coeducation, faculty members worked on developing neutral language in instruction, in policies, and in promotional materials. The emphasis on language was not surprising since the faculty had read and discussed Deborah Tannen's (1990) popular book, *You Just Don't Understand*. Neutral and inclusive language reflected the common denominator in faculty thinking about what was fundamental to an environment that promotes sex equity. Even those traditional teachers who were not convinced that coeducation was a good idea agreed that they needed to eliminate female "put-downs" in their language.

Discipline and management: a gentler, kinder classroom

Staff and faculty described Xavier as a high quality, prestigious college-prep school with high-caliber, well-rounded students who worked hard. Several teachers reported that discipline practices helped them create a strong academic learning environment. With the introduction of young women, many teachers expected to have a few weeks of disruptive, rude male behavior, harassment, or female flirtatious behavior, but they believed that by holding firm they would ride the tide of any unforeseen troubles. Many expected young women to be less rowdy in class and less tolerant of inappropriate student behavior, thereby having a positive effect on classroom discipline.

WHAT YOUNG WOMEN WILL BRING TO CLASSROOMS

Teachers saw young women as "humanizing," "open," more "willing to talk," and more "personally revealing" in class. Some teachers believed young men felt uncomfortable with personal disclosure and that the presence of young women would create a more accepting environment for sharing personal experiences. Conversely, a few teachers viewed personal disclosure as a negative phenomenon; they felt the presence of young women would jeopardize their ease in interacting with young men in a direct, confrontational style.

DO FEMALES AND MALES NEED DIFFERENT RULES?

Some faculty and staff wondered if they needed to establish different rules or consequences for young women. One teacher thought that staff might "be more likely to protect the females and that the males might think this is unfair." For example, one staff member asked, "How will it fly when some girl is dressed up and has to pick up garbage for discipline?" Another teacher wondered, "I don't know what I'll do when the first girl cries in my classroom." Some faculty and staff expected young women might respond differently to the rules and to disciplinary consequences when rules are broken. Several staff talked about the inappropriateness of disciplining young women in the harsh, demeaning "tough coach" manner some faculty employed with young men.

As some of the staff had never worked with young women, they felt unprepared to deal with some of the anticipated behaviors. While they hoped the same rules would be appropriate because what was good for young men would be good for young women, they simultaneously held a paradoxical position – that young women may not be the same as young men.

MALE STUDENT BEHAVIOR IN THE PRESENCE OF FEMALES

A few faculty expressed concern that male students were inadequately prepared for the entrance of young women; they feared the males would be self-conscious, "show off," and be more rowdy. One teacher noted, "the male students want to impress the young women, act cool, and tell jokes. I hope I will not have more disruptions when the young women are here." Other staff noted concern about demonstrations of disrespect for females. For example, during one previous visit by young women some young men blocked the bathroom door making "hubba hubba" noises. A female teacher remarked, "Young men are heat seeking missiles." Other female and male teachers worried about the "attitude berating young women as less intellectual," and felt that more work should be done in preparing young men to welcome young women as equals in the classroom. Most teachers, however, believed that the presence of young women would have a positive effect. For decades, the idea of young women creating a "kinder, gentler" educational environment has, in fact, inspired a number of all-male schools to convert to coeducation (Dale, 1969, 1971, 1974).

Patterns of interaction: equal access for young men and young women

Only a few teachers considered that patterns of classroom interaction would require them to monitor student talk and male verbal dominance, especially in small-group work. These few teachers were familiar with the literature revealing that teachers call upon females less frequently than males, and reward females for being neat rather than intellectually curious (Sadker and Sadker, 1994). Some teachers knew that social hierarchies and power to which females are not privy often pervade classroom structures. These few teachers understood how male privilege was embedded in the culture at Xavier. While they described it, and even complained about it, they did not have the skills to counteract the prevailing culture in a more affirmative way.

Extra-Curricular Activities: Athletics and Clubs

Xavier is committed to being a community of learners, and students are strongly encouraged to participate in the larger community and assume leadership in extra-curricular activities; about 85 percent of students were engaged in such activities in the all-male Xavier as well as the coeducational Xavier. Sex equity in athletics, in fact, took up the lion's share of time and resources in the preparation for coeducation. Xavier had a rich history of athletic success and they wanted to create similar opportunities in sports for incoming young women. The school hired new staff to coach women's athletics, and installed a new women's locker room. An in-house joke was that a female teacher had jogged the awareness of the architectural team by asking whether the plans for the new locker room included hair dryers. The original plans had not.

Some faculty hoped young women would organize cheerleading; the current "rag-tag" volunteer squad of male cheerleaders often embarrassed staff. They hoped for a more polished cheerleading squad since sports are such an important part of the image of the high school. As it turned out, the cheerleading squad – composed mostly of young women – did become "more polished" to the deep resentment of some of the returning "rag-tag" males.

In addition to sports offerings, students at Xavier can join any of twenty clubs including peer helpers, National Honor Society, Amnesty International, foreign language, science, and other special interest clubs. Generally students accepted their peer's interests in any of these activities, though athletics did prevail. Teachers expected, and their expectations were realized, that female involvement would enhance clubs such as drama and chorus, which proved to be the case. Several staff noted concerns about the seemingly unequal opportunities for young women in student government. In fact, student body and class elections during the first year of coeducation occurred in the fall (rather than the prior spring) in order to enable incoming students to run for offices. However, the student body officers remained entirely male.

Teacher Adaptability to Innovation

Xavier teachers behaved consistently with the research on the psychological processes of teacher adaptation to innovation as explicated by Hord et al. (1987). Teachers' concerns focus on their own classroom management behavior at first rather than on information seeking and adaptation (Brody, 1993, 1998). They are more concerned about their own adaptability than they are about student outcomes; more concerned about their teaching than about students' learning. But after teachers become clear about "what will happen" and they have had some experience with the innovation, they can shift their focus to students. Once teachers adopt an innovation as "doing business as usual," the change has become institutionalized (Fullan, 1991). Xavier teachers, with a strong sense of efficacy, believed they were ready to face this change competently. Most expressed concern for how to proceed with processes and tasks, and the best use of time, management, and organization. At first, they focused on making necessary adjustments in their classroom management, but they did not want to change too much. Because their level of gender consciousness was operating primarily at Position 1, at eliminating sex bias, they constructed simple expectations about what would happen in their classrooms.

The Outcome: Xavier as a Coeducational School

Virtually all teachers wanted to create a good learning environment for all students and they believed that by eliminating sex bias and treating young women as they had treated young men, they would create a high school that would afford equal educational opportunity to all. And that is what they did. The school culture, pedagogy, the curriculum, and extra-curricular activities, especially sports, looked remarkably the same as they had in previous years. Young women did have the "softening and civilizing" effect on the school; language did change, male rowdy energy was more tempered, and more arts-focused clubs and activities appeared. Yet young women at Xavier looked remarkably like the young men at Xavier: academically talented and motivated, good athletes, leaders of their peers, mostly white, and middle to upper-middle class.

Our analysis of the surveys and faculty group interviews conducted during the first year of coeducation revealed that expectations – both positive and negative – were realized. The transition to coeducation held few surprises. What teachers expected is what they saw happen. We looked at the pre-interview and post-survey data of thirty-seven faculty members (coding provided anonymity but allowed tracing of individuals) and found high correlation between how an individual expected things to happen and how she or he reported what did happen. Those who expected young women to join in and adhere to the same standards as the young men saw little difference in their classrooms and in the school. Those who welcomed the presence of young women as offering something different from the all-male environment focused on the benefits of coeducation; they noted a more humane environment and reported that young women improved the behavioral climate, met or exceeded the academic standards, brought more creative energy to clubs and school activities, were articulate, and contributed depth to class discussion.

Not all expressed a positive view. Some faculty members, as well as some students, blamed females for an erosion of academic standards. Other teachers were perplexed because young women did not respond to the same treatment as young men, and they didn't know what to do about it. For instance, in some classes young women did not participate in the classroom discussions and those teachers did not know how to encourage them to do so. In other classes young women made creative adaptations to homework assignments and teachers were perplexed about how to evaluate these creative endeavors.

Yet, by and large, the faculty and administrators expressed surprise about the smooth transition to coeducation. They wanted to eliminate sex bias and provide the same educational opportunities for young women as they had provided for young men. And they saw themselves as successful.

Not all teachers believed sex equity had been achieved. During small-group faculty interviews, a few expressed doubts about the transition to coeducation. Both male and female teachers with varied years of teaching experience articulated examples of sex bias, particularly affecting female faculty, such as some male faculty members harassing and patronizing younger women faculty. Some, focusing on students, worried that many faculty and administrators remained blind to how their conceptions of gender affected their teaching and their classroom management. A few teachers described the increasing silence of some young women in classes, noting that young women tended to watch and not participate and that while the young women were excellent students, they were determined to assimilate and not make waves. While a few young women students challenged sex bias, for example, by openly calling into question the all-male authors they were reading in their English classes, others spoke privately to teachers after class about the less-than-inviting classroom climate in which male voices increasingly dominated. Some teachers believed that other teachers and counselors needed to better understand young women's development. However, even those teachers who were aware of the effects of beliefs about gender seemed perplexed about what to do about them in their own classrooms, or how to engage other teachers in discussion. They hesitated to bring up issues that many of their peers were tired of talking about, and they were reluctant to raise concerns with the Xavier administration. This group of teachers viewed their administrators as more interested in masking over issues than addressing them – just so the transition to coeducation would go smoothly.

Concerned teachers asked such difficult questions as: What changes should occur in a traditional curriculum that had been developed predominately for white, Western, adolescent males? How could the Xavier faculty teach for better understanding of the roles of men and women? How could they foster more respect between the young men and women? How might they create more respect for individuals from different races, of both sexes, from different social classes, with different interests and abilities in a school where it appeared on the surface that most students were alike?

A Gender Conscious Critique

We think Xavier faculty members largely underestimated or ignored the effects of gender on learning environments by focusing on reducing sex bias (Position 1) and not on seeing how gender is embedded in everyone's thinking (Position 2) and sensing the need for critical transformation (Position 3). Faculty members believed what was good for young men would be good, too, for young women; they had not transformed their thinking beyond welcoming women into the classrooms and maintaining a school culture with a long and honored Ignatian tradition. A curriculum that has traditionally served males well, however, may not serve females equally well. And, in a transformed social order, that curriculum may not even be good for males. Traditional content, structures, and methods that have been championed for young men cannot supply young women with aspirations, explanations, frameworks, and models for their future lives. The young women who arrived at Xavier, like the young women who were smuggled into all-male public high schools in the late nineteenth century, demonstrated they too were adaptable, open, willing, and able to meet the male-oriented standards successfully (Tyack and Hansot, 1990). We would argue, however, that the pedagogy that had been designed for young men, over the course of hundreds of years, is based on the unspoken assumption that white, privileged male is a valued standard for everyone. Such a curriculum potentially places females' adult futures at risk, socializing them to accept sincerely their less privileged position in society.

Although the faculty members at Xavier had five years to plan the change to coeducation, very few of them conceived of their traditional curriculum and their assumptions about the nature of knowing as subject to question. Precisely because of the success of their elite position in the hierarchy of schooling in their community, Xavier faculty members presumed that disciplinary knowledge and curriculum did not need changing. After all, Xavier already had the best of curricula in their minds. They chose instead to focus on managerial aspects of the transition, assuming that substantive changes were unnecessary. We do not offer this critique of the Xavier faculty members in order to lay blame but to point out how their level of gender consciousness and privilege affected how they thought about femaleness and maleness. The values of traditional, essential knowledge to prepare the privileged to become future leaders also creates a ceiling where certain critical questions cannot be asked because no one dares to challenge the paradigm of "excellence."

Their educational philosophy, school mission, and beliefs about the nature of knowledge framed the way Xavier faculty and staff members planned for coeducation and how they assessed the success of their first year. They aimed to eliminate sex bias, were preoccupied with smoothing the bumps in classroom and school management, and were quite pleased the transition went along so well. They were able to subdue masculine bravado and pride in the Xavier tradition and to render the young men neutral enough so that the young women would feel welcomed and so that Xavier could continue to boast about a cohesive community and a traditional curriculum that provides a superior education for "leaders who are men and women for others."

Note

1   Charlene Wilson referred to herself as "Mrs." as a matter of personal choice and institutional norms.

3 Three Teachers, Three Classrooms, Three Schools

Research on single-sex and coeducational schooling has seldom included detailed descriptions of high school classrooms in action. Even more rare have been accounts in which researchers and teachers collaborate in the research process. In the study reported here, each of three researchers paired with a teacher at each of three schools, one a history teacher, one an English teacher, and one a math teacher. Each researcher conducted repeated classroom observations to document classroom interactions. Following extended researcher–teacher conversations about the data gathered, each researcher constructed a classroom portrait of the teacher and students she observed. In this chapter, we present these portraits.

Through observing the teachers interacting with their students, we hoped to see how these teachers' assumptions about gender played out in their curricular and pedagogical decisions. Each researcher had spent several years teaching in public or private K-12 schools, and many years working with novice teachers to develop effective classroom practices. Considerations of how sex and gender might affect classroom dynamics held a fascination for each of us.

The three of us realized from the outset that a complex set of variables can affect teacher behavior, such as: the mix of students for a particular year, the teacher's history and beliefs, and the school's assumptions, expectations, and philosophy that constitute the institutional context. We observed the three teachers in only one context – their classrooms; yet our observations, provided us with rich data that informed our emerging understandings about gender consciousness and privilege. Indeed, many stories from the three classrooms became short-hand anecdotes for summarizing our research findings. The three teachers profiled in this chapter offer a window on our understanding of how individuals express gender consciousness within differing school cultures and how gender consciousness manifests itself in a school. Identifying and defining the concept of gender consciousness across three sites allowed us to compare and contrast how school culture may have influenced the ways in which each teacher defined gender consciousness and acted upon this definition within the classroom.

We did not select the three teachers randomly. Rather, we chose them because students and peers uniformly respected them, identifying them as excellent teachers, and because they welcomed us into their classrooms. In addition, their respective principals recognized them as strong teachers, as leaders among their peers in content knowledge and instructional effectiveness. Principals at the two previously single-sex schools characterized the selected teachers as highly likely to be successful teaching both sexes despite the fact that previously they had taught only in single-sex schools: Brock Bronson had taught young women only and Charlene Wilson had taught young men only. All three teachers wanted to learn more about creating positive learning experiences for their students, and they expressed interest in the consequences of changing from single-sex to coeducation. Finally, the teachers' colleagues viewed them as "progressive" within their fairly traditional Catholic school contexts. The two female teachers identified themselves as feminists. The male teacher, in the previously female single-sex high school, advocated hands-on, experience-based math instruction and believed it would work as well for males as it had for females. In many respects, these three teachers represented "best cases" in their schools of practices reflecting an ethic of care about and fair treatment of students.

Glennellen Pace visited Charlene Wilson's English classes at Xavier Preparatory through the change from male-only to coeducation. Celeste Brody's observations of Nancy North's world history classes at St. Elizabeth's provided a comparison with a school that remained all-female. Kasi Allen Fuller's descriptions of Brock Bronson's coeducational pre-calculus class at Grove Catholic High School gave us a sense of how the introduction of young men to a previously all-female environment might affect curriculum and classroom practice. In what follows, each researcher describes a class session in the life of the teacher she studied.

Sex Equity in a School Designed for Young Men: Charlene Wilson's Coeducational English Class (Researcher, Glennellen Pace)

I drive into the large parking lot at Xavier Prep, ample for the 500-student all-male school I visited last year. But on this October day the lot overflows following the move to coeducation and a 40 percent increase in the student body. The two-minute walk from the parking lot takes me along the periphery of the 56-acre campus through a rose-bordered path leading to the building where Charlene Wilson has taught all-male English classes for five years. I am eager to see and talk with her about the changes on this first visit with her since Xavier became coeducational.

Entering the locker-lined hallway, I am struck by how crowded it seems. Young men and young women stand in clusters talking together and exchanging books from their lockers. I dodge moving arms and squeeze through the crowd to enter Mrs. Wilson's room. Dressed in characteristic slacks and knit turtle-neck top, she turns away from the board where she is writing the agenda for today's class and greets me with the observation, "It's harder to get through the halls this year because students cluster to socialize."

Light pours into the classroom through the nearly floor-to-ceiling, shade-bare windows, drawing my attention to the walls, painted white some time ago, now decorated with a few student "posters" defining and providing examples of literary devices such as onomatopoeia, irony, paradox, metaphor, rhyme, consonance. Along one wall a small bookshelf contains a tumble of assorted paperbacks. Front and center, facing students' desks, sits Mrs. Wilson's desk piled up with books and papers. This stark physical ambiance contrasts with Mrs. Wilson's personal approach to students. Rarely cracking a smile, and with wry humor, she often engages with them in comfortable banter. Clearly she cares for her students and they like her, although she maintains a business-like posture and playfully confrontational style that she herself labels as "male."

As students enter the classroom, they engage in lighthearted exchanges with Mrs. Wilson similar to what I saw prior to the advent of young women, though I notice an absence of hand slapping and other "rough and tumble" physical behavior. Mrs. Wilson comments about this change, confirming that "gentler" behavior is now the norm.

I observe an accelerated freshman English class. In contrast to the male majority in her sophomore class that has just ended, this freshman class has fifteen young women and nine young men. With desks arranged in seven rows of four seats each, the nine young men cluster together in the two rows of desks furthest from the door (rows six and seven), with the ninth young man taking the back seat of the fifth row. Apparently, students have rigidly adhered to this dividing line since school opened in September. On this particular day, however, a young woman takes the back seat in row six. With row five already filled, this forces one young man to sit in a previously all-female row. Mrs. Wilson refers to this as "the continental divide" and openly tells students she thinks it is "pretty humorous." She acknowledges the situation today, "Well, I see Pam has moved across the invisible barrier today. As a result, Mike has reluctantly moved across the barrier, too."

Lisa suggests, "We should rearrange the seating entirely; mix boys and girls just to see if we could survive." No one responds to this suggestion.

Mrs. Wilson presents today's agenda, and talks about an upcoming test and an assignment in conjunction with their reading of *Old Man and the Sea*. The assignment, to create a journal entry in which they represent their ideas visually rather than verbally, confounds some students. Mrs. Wilson wants the highly verbal students to stretch beyond their comfort zones to represent their ideas in alternative ways.

"I know it's difficult; more so for some of you," begins Mrs. Wilson.

Anne asks, "What if you can't draw the way you think?"

"Then find another way to represent things visually. For example, a diorama is a visual representation. This is not an art project. I just want you to represent your ideas visually. I'm going to have to ask you to go along with me on this for awhile. I'm asking you to venture into unfamiliar territory." Mrs. Wilson probes: "Why do you think I am not giving you more precise instructions? Why do you think the assignment is vague?"

Students chat with each other about her question, suggesting reasons such as: "You want to see how many different things we come up with?"

Satisfied that they better understand the expectations for the visual journal, Mrs. Wilson gives students seven minutes to prepare for a discussion about *Old Man and the Sea*. They write questions they have and draw a picture to represent the difference between Hemingway's style in this story and Steinbeck's style in *Of Mice and Men*, which they have read previously.

Mrs. Wilson then indicates they'll have a whole-class discussion. "You need to have your visual journal, your questions, your books and something to write with, and quickly, quietly round it up." The class calmly and efficiently pulls the desks into a circle, young women on one side and young men on the other, maintaining the "divide." Mrs. Wilson begins circulating a paper, asking students to select and write down one question each from their individual lists. While the paper moves around the circle, she asks for volunteers to share their pictures.

Carole shares her drawing. She receives no response. Bob says he will talk about but not show his drawing, explaining that he did not create one in class today since he already had one stored in his accordion file – a file of student-selected work – "because it was a memorable piece." He describes a dot-to-dot Christmas Tree. Colin says, "It was really neat." Betty shares, but, as with Carole, receives no response. Martin shows his drawings, a peaceful setting for Steinbeck, a city scene for Hemingway and Mrs. Wilson prompts him to explain why. Don shares his pictures, "This represents terseness for Steinbeck, and for Hemingway I drew a woman who is beating around the bush."

Many students visibly react. Several female students hasten to say it could just as well be a guy who beats around the bush. Don says he didn't mean it as a "woman-only" thing. At this point, Mrs. Wilson interjects that although Don didn't intend to employ a female stereotype, nonetheless others might view it that way.

Anne asks why "we have to read two books, one of them very sexist and the other with no female characters."

Mrs. Wilson responds: "My fault."

Jane pipes up: "Why are we focusing on this point?"

Jeremy begins: "Don't get mad at me, but … " at which point Mrs. Wilson interrupts, "Then watch what you say."

Jeremy decides they should move on to someone else to let him rethink the phrasing of his question. He remains visibly introspective as the conversation continues.

James: "I feel like the girls are telling me it's my fault that the author wrote the book that way and that you [Mrs. Wilson] chose it for us to read."

Students and teacher look at one another, but for a moment no one speaks. Then Jeremy's wrinkled brow smooths as he apparently abandons his attempt to rephrase his thought as a question and announces, "The most powerful character in *Old Man and the Sea*, the fish, is female."

The young women talk about how these books are "picking on girls." Jane repeats several times, "Why should we focus on that?" Anne answers that it is part of the book and they should be able to talk about all aspects of the book. Mrs. Wilson assures students that she has no interest in making the girls feel bad, or making the boys feel bad *about* the girls feeling bad, "but it is an issue in the books and we should talk about it." She adds, though, that part of the problem stems from her "poor curriculum choice." She will "try to rectify that during the year." She realizes the issue will not go away, asking, "Are there any other comments about text sexism in Room 3?" Bob identifies a problem with sexism besides what's in the texts, "because there's a forbidden row [row 5] that people only sit in if there is no place else to sit." Mrs. Wilson explains her reasoning: students should be able to sit by friends, but, she adds, if they want a seating chart she could create one. Jeremy jokingly makes a derogatory comment about females and Mrs. Wilson sends him out of the room. She tells the group they are not to put each other down, not even jokingly.

The conversation continues with several young women commenting that they find the book, *Old Man and the Sea*, confusing. Pam says, "I don't get this. I think the guy is kind of crazy." It's unclear whether Pam refers to the old man in the story or to Hemingway, but no one asks her about this. Young women continue to comment, sharing mixed opinions about the book: "I see something in it that makes it a classic"; "I like the book"; "I don't really get it, but I expect to as we discuss it"; Jennifer suggests: "This seems like a legend – something passed down from generation to generation."

These comments come quickly, one on top of the other. Students appear to be listening and interested, but none of these comments precipitates a discussion.

Mike points out differences in "the way girls and boys understand the story because of differences in the way they relate to the story." He gives examples that he thinks are "more feminine – geared more toward women." Martin picks up on this idea, suggesting additional sex stereotypes that "bring about differences in response to the book." The bell rings, terminating the discussion.

I note that the young women's comments typically did not generate discussion or response, whereas a comment from a male more often stimulated an exchange of ideas. On the other hand, once a comment captured students' interest, young women participated every bit as energetically and vigorously as young men. I recognize, however, that comments from young men often related to sexism, clearly a hot topic for everyone.

Following class, Jeremy re-enters the room to discuss his derogatory remark with Mrs. Wilson and admits he knows that jokes can hurt. Their behavior with one another remains comfortable and friendly, though after he leaves Mrs. Wilson explains to me that Jeremy's older brother has attended Xavier and is antagonistic toward coeducation. She thinks Jeremy feels the same way. "Both," she explains, "are hockey players and fit the image of the rough-type male." Yet, her interpretation of Jeremy's behavior differs from mine. Remembering how he prefaced a comment with, "I don't want you to take this wrong" and carefully phrased his ideas so others would understand his intentions, I think Jeremy wanted to grapple with the issues of sexism but had little language or skill to do so.

Mrs. Wilson, pleased with the content of the class discussion, admits, "I guess I'm going to have to make some changes in the curriculum sooner than I thought I would. I didn't change the books I use for this year partly because I'm working on my master's degree and I'm too busy, but also because I thought these books were fine. But the students are pushing for more gender-balanced materials. I'll tell you, I never had this discussion last year. Except for my pointing out these aspects of the books, issues of sexism were largely not discussed. Now, this is a central focus of students' discussions."

Analysis and Interpretation

The classroom context

Charlene Wilson identifies herself as a feminist; her colleagues see her as one who speaks her mind and expects others to listen to her and other women faculty. She has taught only males during her entire teaching career and has developed her teaching style accordingly. In her new coeducational classroom, she purposefully tries to use principles of sex equity, and her female students' perceptions about male-defined literature undoubtedly will push her to make curricular choices that include female voices.

In class discussions, Mrs. Wilson pointedly monitors students' comments, allowing no "put downs" even as jokes. She actively demands non-sexist language, and eschews behaviors that might result in any student feeling academically or psychologically unsafe. She guides students to openly examine sex stereotyping in their reading and their conversation; she takes seriously her role in creating a safe atmosphere for young women and young men, and in raising students' consciousness about sex bias. Whereas in all-male classes the previous spring I saw her occasionally ignore sexist comments, during my visits in the first year of coeducation she always responded swiftly, showing students she would not tolerate such comments in her classroom.

The sex-based seating arrangements remained because Mrs. Wilson decided the benefits of student choice outweighed the benefits of teacher-assigned seating and working groups. This did not mean, however, that she had a laissez-faire attitude about gendered relationships. She used her humor to point out the "invisible barrier" and to nudge students to think about their behavior. She grappled with this throughout the year, wondering whether she should intervene or should leave decisions to students who do not realize the impact of gender in their lives.

Mrs. Wilson began the coeducational year with the same books she had used previously. She believed books she had taught from successfully with her all-male classes would serve young women just as well. By October, however, young women voiced their dissatisfaction with what they called sexist material. Mrs. Wilson listened, rethought her position, and acknowledged that she would have to change her curriculum to be more inclusive of female voices.

Charlene Wilson saw changes in classroom discussions with the presence of young women. For example, the previous year in an all-male group discussing "The Lottery," young men talked about women's roles in the story but generally explained women's position in the book as belonging to the past, claiming "today women have a position more equal to that of men." Charlene Wilson, as the only female and with the authority of the teacher, found it difficult to question their presumptions. Young women in the class, however, did not find it a problem to question the presumptions of the males' perceptions of female equality; the presence of young women substantively increased the depth of discussion.

On the other hand, compared with the young women, the young men's comments more often generated responses and discussion, even though this class had nearly twice as many females as males. Entries in Mrs. Wilson's journal, kept throughout the first year of coeducation, noted males consistently received more attention, both positive and negative. Nonetheless, the young women influenced discussions and, ultimately, Mrs. Wilson's curriculum. She said it best:

> I'll tell you, I never had this discussion [regarding *Old Man and the Sea*] last year. Except for my pointing out these aspects of the books, issues of sexism were largely not discussed. Now, sexism is a central focus of students' discussions.

I met with Mrs. Wilson three years after the advent of coeducation. She had expected that the young women would do better in her classes than the young men, because traditionally females have excelled in measures of verbal skills and in English classes. She found her expectation consistent with what happened. However, she had been surprised to see the amount of self-doubt young women expressed as compared to her male students, despite their exemplary performance. Repeatedly, she heard successful young women in her accelerated classes express uncertainty about remaining in the accelerated class track. Not one young man had ever done so; even those who performed marginally would beg to remain in the accelerated track, promising to work harder. She had begun to see patterns of sex difference and how gender as a construct may be a powerful influence on developing males and females.

The institutional context

Colleagues viewed Mrs. Wilson as a "progressive" teacher with student-centered pedagogy. Mrs. Wilson solicited and encouraged students' ideas, invited them to create their own questions and to construct meaning in alternative modes, and held authentic discussions where students could voice their opinions. She validated with comments such as, "That's a good point; I hadn't thought of that before." She used a variety of strategies to optimize student involvement. For instance, she grouped differently for different purposes: in pairs, small groups, a circle for whole-class discussions, a semi-circular theater-style array for skits or readers' theater.

Charlene Wilson consciously sought to teach in student-centered ways which are often associated with feminist views of teaching. In a school where many teachers adopted a more hierarchical, authoritarian, teacher-centered focus in their classrooms, she was different.

But the institutional context in which they find themselves influences what teachers do. Despite Charlene Wilson's focus on her students, and her attempts to achieve sex equity within her classroom, she was bound by the traditions and the authority of the all-male school grounded in a patriarchal system. The traditional definition of curriculum and the strong teacher-as-authority norm constrained her pedagogical repertoire. We recognized that the unseen and unspoken boundaries of male privilege in Mrs. Wilson's school affected what she could do and what she could see as possible, even with her explicit commitment to feminism and her gender consciousness. The privileged position that traditional sources of knowledge and teacher authority held in the Xavier culture often affected Mrs. Wilson's curricular and instructional decisions. On the other hand, during this same period we had no reports about young women in other English classes clamoring for the need to read a female voice; perhaps a testament to the safe learning environment that Mrs. Wilson constructed for students.

Charlene Wilson openly wondered how the shift to coeducation would affect her relationships with students and students' interactions with one another in her classes; she had hoped the arrival of young women would move the school and classrooms toward increased attention to students' voices and diverse perspectives, both male and female. Three years after coeducation, she thought the school was decreasingly inclusive rather than increasingly inclusive. She thought those who were "other" than mainstream were more marginalized. She believed the school had not developed into more gender consciousness, but less. She thought students had less tolerance for diversity – even toward the young men previously labeled "geeks" and "nerds" – who used to find their niche. "Now," she reported, "they withdraw. And the young women all look alike; and they look much like the young men – bright, competitive, academically and athletically successful." She acknowledged Xavier had fulfilled its purpose; what was good for young men was now available for young women. "For young women who want access to a male-dominated world, what is happening does work. They go out at the top."

Affirmation of Femaleness at St. Elizabeth's Academy: Nancy North's Female World History Class (Researcher, Celeste Brody)

I approach St. Elizabeth's Academy with a certain nostalgia since, I, too, am a product of a Catholic high school. The building is reminiscent of old urban schools still found in the United States, a gray stone and red brick building consuming an entire block in the midst of a busy city, absent of athletic fields or parking lots. Sister Mary Catherine in the front office greets me as I enter the building. A mother-helper carves out a small niche in the entry corridor to work on projects for the students. She shows off the senior quilt that she is stitching together, an annual tradition celebrating the uniqueness of each graduating girl; a work of art, she explains she is proud to help complete it.

Traveling the twenty-five short yards to Nancy North's classroom at the end of the first floor hall, I pass a caucus of African-American students circled tightly in the middle of the corridor holding a meeting, heads bent in serious discussion. Another small group of young women at their lockers, passing the last moments before classes begin, graciously greet me. I note their diverse attire: one is covered in a black lace dress and combat boots with contrasting white face and deep red lips, reminiscent of a Chelsea girl from the 1920s. Another angular young woman stands confidently in outdoor-type garb – flannel shirt, jeans and sandals, topped off with stylish make-up. The infectious energy in the hallway lures me to dally with the young women.

Nancy North's World History Class

Ms. North's classroom typifies those found in old schools. Tan shades cover full-length windows so students aren't distracted by the sights of the city outside. Blackboards line one side, windows another; in the back corner Ms. North stations her desk and computer. Desks arranged in rows will soon be moved for student groupwork and consulting.

Young women stop by the computer to check their current course grade. An African-American student in "office" attire – nylons, neat skirt and sweater – takes attendance. She appears confident in her role and moves around the room with authority. In contrast, the other young women, almost all of whom are white, wear the practical attire of winter: jeans and sweaters or sweat shirts. Glancing over the twenty young women talking quietly among themselves while strung casually on desks or in chairs facing one another, I note the down-to-earth demeanor of everyone in the class, including Ms. North. She, too, wears slacks and a sweater, distinguished from her students only by age and manner of authority. Today she sips an espresso from the corner coffee shop; as the young women enter, she banters with them about their winter holiday adventures.

In this sophomore and junior level world history course, Ms. North "pulls them through" the 100 Years War and the European Crusades. She allows students to make decisions about the rhythm of the curriculum. For instance, students choose at what point they will see a movie – before or after their research paper is due. This morning's class will watch selections from an old version of the movie *Robin Hood* to have a closer view of what a long-bow actually looks like and how it operates. Nancy North emphasizes the effect that new technology has on the outcomes of a war, in this case, on the tiny English army's ability to triumph over the French during the wars that follow. Students are sick of the crusades, she chuckles, but they must have a test yet on this material. She expects them to write their own test questions today, an activity they will take seriously.

Ms. North explains her larger purposes in teaching this survey course:

> History is a tool for putting things together; it is creating the story of the past. I teach it as if I am telling a story and the young women are part of that process – putting the pieces together to make a whole way of understanding. History also provides material for doing research. Unless these young women are going to be historians, they don't need to remember the details. They do have a research project that requires a working thesis and argument.

Ms. North has reviewed students' first drafts to help them locate their thesis. "The reason I do this research paper requiring a thesis statement is that when they go to college they will be asked to write a four page paper. I want them to be ready. My goal is that they should then find college easy."

She requires three drafts of the paper; two individual edits and one peer edit. She constantly revises existing, standardized material for young women so that they can see the effects of sex bias, and see themselves as actors in the world of research.

She has modified a Michigan State University handout for doing a research paper to fit a "girl's point of view," changing the examples so the young women can relate. Her humor is evident when she makes a point on her citation; on the board behind her is a made-up example of the proper form for citations: "North, Nancy. *Woman and Superwoman*. Seattle, Washington: Saint Elizabeth's Books, 1994." The young women see it and laugh.

The Middle Ages is Ms. North's favorite period of history; it directs her own travel and research around Europe. She shares numerous historical anecdotes as she weaves the story with the young women. She uses film to capture the atmosphere and compare how the period in which a film was made affects the tone and, consequently, the message; she has an extensive slide library of pictures taken during her travels which she uses judiciously during these presentations.

Ms. North is a seasoned teacher. She began her career in the midwest twenty plus years ago, working in a public school. When she relocated to this city as a single parent, she chose St. Elizabeth's because it was a place where she could remain enthusiastic about teaching. She loves to teach humanities, literature and history. I recognize a confident teacher at ease with herself and clear about her role in preparing her young women for the rigors of college. She speaks with pride about her former students who return from college to confirm that her approach works on their behalf.

"We need to be seated. Ladies, today we will finally construct the crusades test, then watch the Robin Hood movie." Students cluster quickly into groups of three and four without any prompting or fanfare. Accustomed to doing this exercise, they appear to understand the value of it for their performance on the test. Ms. North will select from their essay and multiple choice questions for the upcoming test, so framing a good question has immediate currency for the young women. She also emphasizes that constructing good questions is an attribute of a good historian.

Ms. North adds humorously, "You get to include all those things you know and love."

Students have formed seven small groups, with one group of five creating an amoebae-like circle precariously holding a late arriving student who turns her ear to the group. The recorder in that group calls to Ms. North who has been sitting back waiting for students to ask for her assistance: "Is this all right?"

Ms. North reads their first question, nods, and the girl chuckles to her group, "We are smart!"

Students negotiate their understandings among themselves with full attention: "I remember how ... Eleanor would ... "; "I'm confused about that ... "; "Should we do another multiple choice first?" Some students use texts to locate material. Most conjure questions from their memories. Some check with each other, "Could we say ... ?" while others offer explanations.

Ms. North signals the transition to the next phase of the activity with, "Five minutes more. Essay questions have to be 'why' or 'why not,' not just 'what.'"

One girl playfully challenges another group, "We have two multiple choice and one essay question. Top that."

Ms. North calls the class to attention. "OK. Who wants to go first? Listen up, and when you answer a question try to give your reasons."

Ms. North recognizes student volunteers. "Stand and deliver," she directs. Two young women stand and give a two-minute response to the question they have written, "Holy wars ... ; jihad ... "

Ms. North interrupts, "How did that jihad fit in?" She uses the young women's questions to prompt a brief response from another student to insure understanding of the idea of holy wars.

A student asks, "I have a question. Which was the real first crusade? I mean, the last real one?"

Ms. North: "That's not a good question."

Another girl assists, "You could say, 'Which was the last important crusade?'"

Ms. North: "Good. That's a better question."

The sharing of questions continues. Ms. North makes comments to emphasize specific points. She finally resorts to giving answers to the questions instead of referring them to other students to answer or clarify as a glance at the clock indicates that time is running out for this activity.

A representative from the last group speaks: "Name the four crusades and who led the ... "

Ms. North: "Hang on to this question. Which one was the first ... ? Doesn't anyone remember the Arab phrase for 'It's fate'?"

She writes on the board the Roman numerals: I, II, and III. "Do these crusades accomplish what they set out to do?" A rapid exchange of questions and answers ensues among the young women about the three crusades.

Student: "I have a quick question. It is about the children's crusade. Why don't we hear much about this one, and what happened to the children?"

This question draws rapid side exchanges among the young women, then a student responds: "Because children didn't count!"

Student: "Too bad. If they were women they wouldn't count either!"

Ms. North: "Probably about 10–15 percent of the children went on the crusade. Remember the 'Pied Piper' song? It told the story about the children following the recruiter who came to their village. They followed without question. Imagine the parents letting their children go off and thinking they would come back shortly. After this there are still crusades, but what starts to happen? In the end you open up trade. Intellectuals discover other regions. It opened up a whole new world for Europe and for a while it was almost a renaissance. What happened to women during the crusades? They own land, work more, have their own businesses."

Student: "The men are gone and they cover home, doing everything. Like in World War II and the Civil War."

Ms. North: "It happens after almost every war. The men come back and the women return to what they formerly did. Remember your test is on Friday. Do I have your questions? Do I have every group's questions?"

The mood and desk arrangement changes as the students get ready to continue the movie, *Robin Hood*.

Ms. North begins, "Let me update you." She lectures briefly, reviewing the importance of the long-bow and its significance, describing the size of this bow, how much strength it took to use, and its ability to penetrate armor. This technology changed warfare as it had been experienced to this point in time.

The video continues where they left off from the previous day. With little time before the end of the period, the film climaxes at the scene where the maiden, Marion, is about to be forced to marry the wicked sheriff of Nottingham, John. She intends to resist and contemptuously hurls these words at John, "What you want I have given to another man, with pleasure." The young women clap, cheer and obviously love her defiance in the face of this forced marriage.

The bell rings and the video is turned off. From all corners of the room students offer, "UGH." They want to continue the movie. Two young women repeat in jubilant chorus Marion's famous line, "What you want I have given to another man, with pleasure," offering each other a high five hand shake for emphasis. They leave the room laughing together.

Analysis and Interpretation

When I talked with Nancy North about the students' reactions to Marion, and how often she makes reference to the condition of women and children, I asked, "Do you think it is easier, in general, to deal with women's issues at St. Elizabeth's?"

"Most definitely. For example, I will point out in Shakespeare's play, *Henry Vth*, before we view the scene where the French are preparing for battle with the English, how the men are playing 'mine is bigger than yours.' When the other English teachers at this school teach the play *Romeo and Juliet* they can very openly discuss, 'The moon, inconstant moon,' as this is an explicit reference regarding menstruation."

"Could they have that discussion within a mixed class?" I asked.

"Sure, I have, when I taught in public school, but not with the same emphasis as I can here."

Gender Consciousness and Privilege

Ms. North understood the significance of the standard curriculum and preparing St. Elizabeth's young women for success in college. Consequently, any observer would recognize how preparation for college ordered the formal, explicit curriculum of this classroom. The major themes from world history are discernible to whomever has studied Western history in high school or college: the crusades, the Renaissance and the great wars coupled with the exercise of learning to write well-constructed research papers. I also witnessed, however, how a teacher's notion of history as story, and teaching as creating the narrative, framed the young women's study of the events. This curriculum taught as a critique of the past extended to a critique of present times and would be appropriate for any group of students, whether they proceeded to college or not. For instance, Ms. North emphasized the role of technology in shaping and changing warfare, an idea that is not new, but one that came alive with her skillful use of film and her keen sense of story. A sub-theme was teaching students to view film critically and with an eye to how the culture and social climate create new emphases with old stories.

What stood out dramatically in the classroom text was the steady consciousness regarding gender that both teacher and students gave to the topics from world history using standard texts. The nature of the discourse indicated that previous topics included active discussions about women and their place in history and that future discussions would continue to integrate a conscious feminist perspective despite the fact the texts pay little attention to the role of females. Ms. North provided a purposeful approach to sex inequities and sex differences as well as a consciousness about gender through the curriculum and her instruction at three levels: (1) she altered the traditional curriculum by deliberately pointing to sex inequities and biases inherent in it, (2) she critiqued underlying patriarchal attitudes, and (3) she supported female defiance of male privilege.

Points to sex inequities and biases in the traditional curriculum

Ms. North provided numerous examples of sex inequities and biases in the curriculum and gave affirmation for being female which did not go unnoticed by her students. For example, she modified the text book example of a proper citation which used a male name as an example by using her female name and their school name; she made a point to include females which drew smiles and chuckles from the young women. The humor generated among the students and the teacher indicated that this kind of adaptation happened often. In so doing she pointed out to the students the limitations of traditional and mainstream curricula, and versions of the curriculum.

Critiques patriarchal attitudes

Several examples of Ms. North's conscious critique of male attitudes toward women and toward the world occurred during my observations. Ms. North deliberately prompted the young women to witness Shakespeare's skill in depicting the deeply patriarchal male competitive experience. When she showed the movie version of *Henry the Vth* she stopped the video just before the scene when the French military leaders compared the superiority of their steeds while they anxiously awaited the dawn and battle. She referred to it as "another example of 'Mine is bigger than yours.'" The sexual allusion was not lost on anyone; this was not the first time this phrase had been used. In another school Ms. North might actually be reprimanded for talking about males this way; from a patriarchal point of view her words might be considered a form of male ridicule, but in this setting it was accepted as a feminist point of view.

Openly supports female defiance of male privilege and the treatment of women

Maid Marion's open defiance of her impending forced marriage in the scene from *Robin Hood* and the cheers it drew from the young women was an indication of the ease with which an all-female group could engage in a critique of women's treatment with no resistance or competing explanation. In a later class session, a lengthy student-led discussion of Joan of Arc's tragic ending was another example of how ready and able the young women were to consider the special status of women in historic as well as contemporary times. Ms. North admitted that she had raised the same issues when she taught in the public school, but it was much easier to do this in St. Elizabeth's all-female environment.

During my interviews with Ms. North and in her lectures she openly critiqued the Catholic Church during the Middle Ages. Although other faculty members pointed out that Nancy North was more "progressive" than many of the teachers in the school, her critique of the Church was acceptable in this setting. She had license and support for addressing the issues of sex inequity and patriarchy indicating the level of critique permissible at St. Elizabeth's. She was permitted to raise questions of social inequality in her classroom.

Ms. North conducted a highly interactive instructional environment. Although she held the narrative threads of the course, young women often interjected with "why" questions followed by their own extended elaboration to each other's questions, generating a classroom discourse in which teacher and students continued to create the conversation. Students engaged energetically in developing the story.

Nancy North also demonstrated how a teacher can strike her own balance between a traditional view of curriculum and teacher authority and methods of instruction that insure student engagement. The level of engagement in the small-group work showed she expected students to push one another's thinking. Students took their work seriously and continued the critique when they conducted peer editing of their research papers, and when they crafted questions for their examination.

The St. Elizabeth's culture gave Nancy North a great deal of latitude to critique the status quo, particularly the condition of women, and it supported her compensatory practices for females. Ms. North, however, represented the "progressive" end of St. Elizabeth's faculty; she admitted to being more of a feminist than other teachers. But she felt fully supported in making her views known and in her efforts to create an awareness of women's less privileged position throughout history.

Differing Institutional Contexts

The embedded concepts of gender at St. Elizabeth's differed from those at Xavier. These differing institutional contexts influenced Nancy North and Charlene Wilson. Whereas both wanted to achieve sex equity – each raising issues of bias and discrimination – Nancy North could move further in the continuum to gender awareness; she pointedly and directly raised issues of patriarchy, or women's defiance to male authority.

Nancy North moved beyond achieving sex equity toward the positive affirmation of femaleness. We should point out, she also had a longer teaching career in several different schools. Perhaps she had a wider repertoire of teaching strategies and felt more comfortable with her pedagogical approaches and with changes over the years in expectations for women.

Nancy North and Charlene Wilson both actively address issues of sex differences and gender; they both respect students' voices and help students to find their own meaning. But both of them also teach in the context of college preparatory schools; they must prepare students to be successful in elitist, prestigious universities and they consciously seek to convey the material deemed important to scholarly authorities. Much of that scholarly material does not include female voices.

Unconsciously and Unsuspectingly Sex Equitable: Brock Bronson's Coeducational Pre-Calculus Class (Researcher, Kasi Allen Fuller)

As I make my way through the concrete edifice that is Grove Catholic High School in search of Mr. Brock Bronson's classroom, the hallways virtually bubble with the energy that so often accompanies the first sun-filled days of spring. I am reminded of my own days as a student in an all-female Catholic school, and of my years teaching math in a coeducational Catholic high school.

The students move about quickly from place to place, some literally running. Posters announcing spring activities and potential summer opportunities don the walls. A group of young women giggle in the corner, dressed in a variety of fashionable spring attire: shorts and sneakers, a skirt and sandals, a sundress. A similarly-sized group of young men huddles near the lockers, sporting a sort of "athletic grunge" look; they discuss a band they hope to see over the weekend. Two cheerleaders walk by in uniform and a young couple sneaks a kiss before going off to class. Teachers lean in their doorways as students change classes between periods. The mood is jovial, with students greeting teachers as well as each other.

Mr. Bronson's room typifies the larger building's cement construction. Painted a steel gray-blue color, metal windows constitute one wall and chalkboards cover the remaining three. Mr. Bronson's desk sits at the front of the room. The back corner houses a large metal shelving unit overstuffed with various pieces of physics equipment; he also teaches the school's physics course. With some regularity, one can find a student sitting at the back of the room quietly working with pieces of physics equipment while the math class presses on. The room decor consists primarily of a hand-painted mural – a large pencil that wraps around two of the walls below the chalkboards – rather fitting for a math teacher who discourages his students from working in pen. I recognize a couple of posters from NCTM (National Council of Teachers of Mathematics) containing exclusively mathematical images with no people represented.

After leaning in the doorway a few minutes to supervise students changing rooms, Mr. Bronson often takes a seat at his desk between classes: collecting his thoughts, perusing his notes, organizing papers, and then standing as the time for the bell to ring approaches. Physically speaking, he is a presence to reckon with – a large man, in his early forties, well over six feet tall and fairly bulky. He has large hands with fingers that make the chalk look minuscule; his hair is short, almost of military style, and speckled with gray. He wears cotton trousers and button-front shirts, no tie; his shoes are simple leather oxfords designed for people who spend the majority of each day on their feet. He grins often, but seldom laughs aloud; he has more of a chuckle that comes deep from within. He is serious and confident, possessing a quick wit – never hesitating to poke a little fun at his students. Mr. Bronson appears both widely read and highly capable in mathematics. I recognize immediately how much his students respect him. When I learn that only shortly before coming to Grove Mr. Bronson had left his life as a pastor and priest, I am somehow not surprised.

Mr. Bronson's Pre-Calculus Class

The junior–senior Honors pre-calculus class I observe consists of eighteen young women and four young men. Aside from three female Asian international exchange students, all students appear to be of European descent. Students' seats are arranged in five rows of five, although the seating patterns change depending on the activity. The four young men take seats toward the back; only young women sit in the first rows. The class makes use of a highly acclaimed late 1980s textbook by Paul Forester that emphasizes story problems and mathematical modeling.

As the class begins, Mr. Bronson first "checks in" on a few of the home-work review problems relating to the previous day's topic – exponential functions. He asks for volunteers to "nicely present" a couple of the prob-lems, encouraging them to "take a helper if you want." Four students volunteer – three young women and a young man, all Caucasian. They write their solutions to three problems on the board: one young woman works alone, the young man works alone, and two of the young women work together. As the volunteers present their answers, Mr. Bronson makes the rounds and addresses individual student concerns. One young man asks for more practice with a particular type of problem – similar to the one the two young women will explain. A number of students raise similar concerns during the student presentations. Mr. Bronson responds positively, and when the volunteers have finished, he relates their question to a chemistry applica-tion. A discussion of pressure and boiling points ensues. Mr. Bronson brings up an example about the boiling point of blood which the students calculate to be 98.6 degrees Fahrenheit at 60,000 feet prompting immediate squeals of "Eew!" from the young women and "Cool!" from the young men. Mr. Bronson just smiles. If he has noted the sex-based difference in his students' responses, he likely finds it interesting, but ultimately unimportant. Mathematics is his mission.

As students recover from the blood problem, Mr. Bronson turns to today's topic – ellipses. "OK, everybody, get a partner and a string and tie a loop." Students ask if they can have three to a group or if they can work alone. "Let's try for pairs," Mr. Bronson suggests. "You're going to need at least three hands to do this." Students begin moving their desks in order to facilitate the work of pairs and trios. It takes a few minutes for them to get settled.

To speed the process, Mr. Bronson tells them, "Today, I want you to show me how to make an ellipse. You'll need three pencils. I've got extras if you need them." He begins to mill around, helping students get to work. After about three minutes, he asks, "Does everyone have an ellipse?" Two young women are having trouble because they've placed their pencils too close together. He asks a question; the students adjust their pencils in response. "That's it," he encourages them.

"I want to see a long skinny one now. Let's try to make one that looks like a cigar – a Cuban cigar." Another group (also two young women) calls out, "Uh-oh, our string is stretching," to which Mr. Bronson replies, "Yeah, looks like we've got cheapo string. You've got the right idea though. Do the best you can." Mr. Bronson makes the rounds and checks with each group to see that they have made some adjustment in their original ellipse in order to make it thinner.

"Now," he pulls the group together, "let's take out your notes and write down a few things about what you just did ... or at least attempted to do." He smiles and most students chuckle along with him. "What were you holding down just now?" A female student answers, "the foci."

Mr. Bronson proceeds to lead the group through a series of questions that encourage the students to connect their hands-on experience of constructing the physical model of an ellipse with the more theoretical diagram he has drawn on the board. Throughout this discussion, all of the female students in the class are writing, all of the male students are sitting and listening but not writing. The conversation moves quickly. The female students write, answer questions, nod, refer back to notes from a previous day, ask a question, write some more. The young men tend to watch, nod, and ask questions more than they answer them. The discussion is rich.

Mr. Bronson's ability to bring in details, either ideas from other fields or finer points that will preempt common misconceptions, surpasses that of most teachers I have observed. The class talks about the Latin meaning of the word foci, the connection between ellipses and circles, how the Pythagorean Theorem relates to all of this. Mr. Bronson continuously throws out questions. Students have a tendency to call out both answers and questions during this portion of the class. The voices heard calling out loudest generally belong to the four young men. Mr. Bronson takes some of their suggestions but actually calls primarily on young women, most of whom are raising their hands. Students also freely add on to each other's answers. Interspersed between questions and answers is lots of laughter. These students appear to love being here.

The presentation and discussion continue. Mr. Bronson explains, "There is one number that we haven't talked about yet." And he writes, "Definition," on the board. "But first, Anna, I'm going to put you on the spot. Why did Kepler pick Mars to study orbits?" She answers fairly directly, "Because it was the most elliptical?" "And therefore?" Mr. Bronson asks. "The most eccentric," she adds.

"Let's talk about eccentricity," he suggests, and begins a series of unfinished statements that he asks students to complete. Students call out answers, almost as a group. At times, he asks questions of specific students. For example, to one male student who has been especially vocal, he addresses the question: "Why is 'e' (eccentricity) always less than one?" The student cannot answer. Instead, a handful of female students offer their suggestions. "Actually," Mr. Bronson concludes, "it's because all of the most exciting things happen between 0 and 1. OK, seriously, let's generalize." Again, this task occurs through an interactive process reflecting the Socratic method. However, Mr. Bronson always states the question before calling on the student.

"Where are we the most eccentric? [pause] Beth, what do you think? Where are we the least eccentric? [pause] Anna, can you help us? What about those cigars; what do you think about their eccentricity? [pause] Linda, you and Marie made a perfect Cuban cigar shape. How about a paper clip? [pause] Joe? How about a circle? [pause] What can we say about its eccentricity, Wendi?"

Mr. Bronson controls the dissemination of knowledge in large part, but at the same time he provides students with opportunities to make sense of the mathematics based upon their own experience. Through class activities and discussions, he insures that each student has the chance to articulate individual understandings of mathematical ideas.

At this point, Mr. Bronson shifts to specific problems. "Let's try analyzing a few actual ellipses," he suggests. "I know you're dying to do this." Mr. Bronson writes an equation on the board and begins, "OK, what do we know?" A male student volunteers the first piece of information. The remaining volunteers are female. After graphing the ellipse, Mr. Bronson suggests they "try a messier one." He asks Erica where the y-intercepts would be. "Like, maybe, 8?" she responds doubtfully. "Like, maybe, where? Could you try giving me that answer again?" he smiles with a knowing look. Erica gathers her thoughts for a moment. "Well, they would have to be at +8 and −8, because those are the values when x is zero," she comes back at him. "That's right," he affirms. In the course of the students' ensuing discussion, they catch him in a mathematical error and all clap with pleasure. He laughs.

Next, Mr. Bronson gives students an opportunity to try one of the graphs on their own. Most work independently. Two pairs of young women and one coed pair work together. After a few minutes, Mr. Bronson checks in with the group as a whole, "We need 'c.' What's the easy way?" Three female students chime in; two are holding calculators. "Calculators no, heads yes," Mr. Bronson responds. "How about finding the eccentricity without a calculator?" All students in Mr. Bronson's upper division classes are required to have scientific calculators. He is, however, an avid supporter of "mental math" and tries to educate students about what he deems appropriate calculator use. Together class members review how to calculate eccentricity.

Meanwhile, Mr. Bronson has asked two female students to draw their graph on the board, while students remaining in their seats compare their results. Only a few minutes remain in the period, but Mr. Bronson makes use of each and every one. "Let's do a little mental math magic trick." The students seem eager to join him. Even Jonathan, who has spent much of the period muttering sarcastic comments and has already begun packing his belongings, stops to take part. "No pencils, or paper, or calculators, just these," he says, tapping his temple with his index finger. "Pick a number between one and ten," Mr. Bronson instructs. He then leads the students through a series of steps involving seemingly every mathematical operation, including squares and square roots. When all of the students end up with their original numbers, one of the young men asks, "Did you get this out of *Reader's Digest* or something?" Mr. Bronson responds, "Let's talk about what I'm doing and see if we can represent it algebraically. When I ask you to pick a number between one and ten, I'm really just saying … ?"

"Take any x!" a female student calls out.

"Right!" says Mr. Bronson, writing an "x" on the board behind him.

The group continues to represent the trick algebraically. "Hey, you just made a perfect square," a female student chimes in. "Let's do another one," says a second young woman. The group seems to nod in agreement. Mr. Bronson starts in again, although there really is not enough time. After seven operations, one of the young women stops the group, "Wait! I just got a remainder." The group is spent and they all break into laughter, including the young woman. "Do you have an answer?" the girl sitting next to me asks a female student nearby. "Isn't it time to go yet?" yells Jonathan from the back row. Turning to their homework, Mr. Bronson says, "It'll have to wait. But I love you too much to let you vegetate tonight." Students sigh and moan, an apparently conditioned response.

Two young women explain that they have a big history paper due tomorrow. Mr. Bronson responds jokingly, "But there's no content in history. You've just got to talk for a long time, right? … Hmm … I'll tell you what. We'll work on this tomorrow. But you owe me big time." There are whispered shouts of "Yes!" and "All right!" The students exit with most of the female students stopping to say, "Thank you, Mr. Bronson." No male student stops to chat with him.

Analysis and Interpretation

One cannot help but learn something about mathematics sitting in Mr. Bronson's class. He embodies the kind of teacher that you wish all students could experience and early enough in their educational career that it might really make a difference. Mr. Bronson uses rather traditional instructional approaches. But his highly structured classes, arguably teacher-centered, remain surprisingly student-focused. More important, his classes stand out as highly sex equitable. Mr. Bronson's refusal to accept behavior and language that might reinforce societal stereotypes about women and mathematics combined with his inclusive classroom strategies set his classes apart from the norm. Ironically, Mr. Bronson claims not to think about issues of sex or gender. In fact, when we first communicated about including his class in this chapter, he sent the following written response:

> In all honesty, I have given no thought to gender issues in the classroom. I was a church pastor for eleven years, and you just learn to treat

everyone equally, I guess. I am either so obtuse that I fail to see what is truly important, or I have totally succeeded at putting gender issues to the sidelines. To me, it is a non-issue (in my classroom). If you still want to talk, at least you've been warned. I probably won't give you much material! I spend all my time improving my own math skills and then trying to communicate my excitement in math to my students.

Brock Bronson, letter dated 3/7/96

This is the same man who, when a female student began to hesitatingly answer a question with, "I don't know if this is right, but … " gently interrupted with, "Am I going to have to give you that lecture again?" The student smiled, blushing slightly, and responded with a far more confident answer.

In addition to Mr. Bronson's classroom, I observed sixty other math classes in five different schools for my dissertation research. Only Brock Bronson appeared to recognize this less-than-confident voice in his female students, acknowledge it and address it. Although Mr. Bronson probably would have responded similarly to a male student exhibiting such self-effacing behavior, I saw only six incidents of males engaging in such self-effacing behavior in the sixty classrooms I observed, whereas I saw fifty-six young women exhibit such behavior out of the fifty-nine observations in which young women were present. Although Mr. Bronson denied any consideration of sex or gender, in the classroom he corrected self-effacing behavior, which females exhibited more than males.

From what I observed, Mr. Bronson succeeded in fostering a sex equitable educational environment – one in which young women and young men could consider options and make decisions based on their own abilities and talents rather than on sex stereotypes, biased expectations, or discrimination. He professed that teachers should treat young men and young women essentially the same, yet he demonstrated sensitivity in his treatment of young women. Whether consciously or unconsciously, he tended to give compensatory treatment to females, perhaps trying to compensate for the sex imbalance and stereotypes so often associated with mathematics. He called on young women more often than young men, chose them more frequently for board work and presentations, and took action to ensure a pervasive and confident female voice in his classroom, quieting the young men from time to time if deemed necessary.

In the following sections I discuss three areas guiding Brock Bronson's pedagogy: (1) his construction of mathemathical meaning, (2) his approach to sex differences and construction of the meaning of gender, and (3) his passion for his subject and for teaching.

Construction of mathematical meaning

Brock Bronson created an empowering classroom environment for learning mathematics. Continuous and varied activity on a daily basis encouraged students to engage fully in the process: posing and answering questions from their seats, solving and presenting problems at the board, and discussing mathematics throughout the period. Almost every class I observed had some mathematical activity that required students to get out of their seats, find a partner, and spend at least a few minutes vocalizing their individual understandings of the mathematics at hand. Mr. Bronson explained some of his motivation:

> We do a fair amount of work at the board. I try to get them up to the board as much as possible so that I can actually see what they're doing. I assign homework every night, but I don't collect it every day. And then we go over it in class. But things slip by me if I don't actually watch them do the problems, so we do that quite a bit.

Mr. Bronson clearly recognized the importance of students individually articulating their mathematical understandings, particularly by presenting to peers via board work. He knew how such opportunities for interaction contribute to the development of students' mathematical knowledge and he provided them frequently.

Approach to sex differences and construction of the meaning of gender

Mr. Bronson admitted he had no particular strategy for assuring that young women learn the most mathematics possible, other than truly trying to treat people fairly and equally. His coed pre-calculus class, however, was markedly different from those of his mathematics colleagues that I observed in the same school. Young women's voices dominated the exchanges in his class and he encouraged females in particular to express their views. Granted, females outnumbered males substantially. However, other teachers, in the interest of making young men feel welcome at Grove, had let male students effectively take over the discourse in their female-majority classes. Mr. Bronson, on the other hand, generally corrected females who contributed apologetically. He did his best to ignore disruptive male behavior, though he did not hesitate to discipline a student if necessary – his least favorite part of the job, he admitted. While he told me at the time that coeducation "really hasn't made a whole lot of difference," he also observed, "The young men are very active and vocal, and they're there, which is different." Still, after teaching only females for seven years, he believed it was "nice to have the guys in there. It makes things a little more balanced, a little more like the real world."

Gender Consciousness and Privilege

Mr. Bronson's extensive experience teaching in the all-female environment had a significant effect on his teaching in the coeducational setting. Teaching female single-sex classes, he grew accustomed to "young women doing everything." He knew well the fine mathematical achievements of young women in his classes. As a result, Mr. Bronson had developed high expectations for female performance and participation that changed little if at all with the advent of male students in his classroom.

Passion for his subject and for teaching

As much as his sense of fairness and long-term experience with female students may have affected his teaching practices, Mr. Bronson's devotion to teaching and his love for his subject combined to make his classroom an exciting place to learn mathematics. When Mr. Bronson and I talked about teaching, he described his greatest enjoyment, "Studying on my own, preparing for class – figuring out the material and how to make it the most accessible – there is really so much that they can understand."

He had taught pre-calculus before and would teach it again. He generally changed examples from year to year to keep things interesting, "but a few years ago," he admitted, "I decided it was time to just dump all of my files and start over – to start fresh."

Mr. Bronson, with a master's degree in mathematics, maintained active professional involvement, publishing in the regional journals for the Mathematics Association of America (MAA) and the National Council of Teachers of Mathematics (NCTM), teaching on weekends, and participating in local and regional conferences. A science teacher as well, his knowledge of chemistry and physics enabled him to bring in dozens of applications to make mathematics relevant for his students. Through him, students could perceive mathematics as a dynamic body of knowledge, a worthwhile pursuit with connections to many other aspects of the world. In addition, they could experience mathematics as fun and engaging, something people can use and learn all their life.

Mr. Bronson's professional activities included membership in the National Council of Teachers of Mathematics (NCTM). Not surprisingly, his classroom reflected general support for the organization's reform-minded Standards for Teaching and Evaluation (NCTM, 1989), which appeared at the end of the 1980s and served as a source of discussion and debate for the past decade. Mr. Bronson challenged his students to learn rather than memorize: to think mathematically, to hypothesize, and to use mathematical discourse. He enhanced this discourse through the use of hands-on activities, student presentations, and board work. In addition, he created a learning environment in which students felt free to take intellectual risks with respect to mathematics. They judged and defended each other's work. They formulated conjectures. Students worked both independently and collaboratively as they explored new mathematical ideas and grappled with new concepts. In short, as Mr. Bronson not only teaches for understanding but does so with fairness and equality, his classroom provided arguably the most positive environment in which young women might learn mathematics that I encountered in this study. Perhaps more importantly, his female students compared to female students in other schools and classrooms reported liking math with more regularity, tested better on standardized measures such as the SAT, and almost all chose to enroll in a fourth year of mathematics even though Grove did not require it for graduation. While it is impossible to determine causality in this particular case, I am quite confident that our society would enjoy far more mathematically literate young women had we more teachers such as Brock Bronson.

Summary

In this chapter we have explored behaviors relating to the gender consciousness of three teachers in three different classrooms in three different schools. These teachers' consciousness of sex and gender differed, revealing different intentions and different consequences for students in their classrooms and school settings.

Nancy North affirmed the meanings of femaleness, actively pointing out gendered cultural norms in the society and in the literature. The two teachers in the newly-formed coeducational schools, Charlene Wilson and Brock Bronson, treated young men and young women equally in that they made sure all students had access to the discourse of the classroom, seeking to implement classroom rules and responsibilities equally and to create safe environments, free of harassment, stereotyping, and sexist language. Charlene Wilson openly admitted her intention to provide sex equity; Brock Bronson claimed no conscious intent although he behaved equitably in practice, in fact providing compensatory treatment to young women.

In all three cases, the institutional context – the school culture – influenced gender consciousness. We observed differences between how teachers constructed gender in single-sex schools as compared with coeducational schools, and in all-female schools as compared with an all-male setting. This led us to ask, how do individuals construct their meanings of femaleness in the different settings? Is femaleness denigrated, ignored, or affirmed?

We found that our female and male single-sex schools differed in this regard. Critiques of male privilege and female affirmation serve as hallmarks in Nancy North's class in an all-female school. As we saw in Charlene Wilson's classes prior to coeducation, within an all-male school the marks of male privilege may go unnoticed, with females ignored in the standard curriculum. With the entry of young women – at least in the safe environment Mrs. Wilson created – female voices and perspectives appeared in the conversations and set the stage for change in curriculum materials, though affirmation of femaleness might remain rare where the male model is still privileged.

Xavier, St. Elizabeth's, and Grove all seek to prepare students for admission to prestigious universities, thus the curriculum across schools tends toward the traditional. But students experienced a different norm about femaleness in the three settings. At Xavier, both as an all-male school and as a coeducational school, males presented the standard model; females strove to emulate that standard. At St. Elizabeth's, students defied and questioned the male model. Teachers at both schools tended to reinforce these patterns. At Grove, teachers and students grappled with the school's ambiguous state, wanting to make young men feel welcome without completely burying Grove's all-female past.

Understandably, Charlene Wilson, a teacher who had not taught young women before Xavier's change to coeducation, could only partially demonstrate her consciousness at the equity level during the first year of the change to coeducation. She wanted to mitigate the effects of the previously all-male environment on young women and stem the presence of sexism sometimes appearing in the young men's comments. The presence of young women created a heightened if somewhat awkward awareness of gender issues among faculty and students. The school had prepared to accept females, but not necessarily to affirm them. For example, Mrs. Wilson's decision not to change her curriculum initially limited her capacity to be gender affirmative. She was skilled enough to probe students' stereotyped comments, and to think about reorganizing the physical environment to challenge the student–peer–culture norms about gender. With more experience, more thoughtfulness about the issues of gender, and an emerging recognition of the need to include female voices and perspectives in her curriculum, Charlene Wilson would become more affirming of femaleness within her classroom. Mrs. Wilson's commitment to sex equity provided a good starting point for her to be open to the information from her female students, and to become increasingly gender conscious.

Brock Bronson posed a particular anomaly because he did not consider himself conscious about sex or gender. His story points out the importance of distinguishing between a teacher's avowed intentions and actual practices. He developed his pedagogy in an environment that encouraged young women to achieve their potential in math, and over time his commitment to equality allowed him to develop strategies that by-passed females' self-doubt, worked through their silence and over-rode other deprecating student behaviors in the classroom. What effect does the intention of the teacher have on whether she or he is considered gender conscious? Mr. Bronson's teaching career evolved during the post-Title IX era with the prevailing norm that high school teachers treat students equally regardless of overt characteristics. Obviously, he was not gender affirmative as was Nancy North at St. Elizabeth's.

For Nancy North's Western civilization course, content was as important as process, and her consciousness extended to the idea that curriculum must be affirmative for young women, providing them with alternative accounts of history and compensatory-type examples to signal the role of women in doing historical research. Nancy North acknowledged that she would have been gender affirmative in a coeducational setting, too, but the all-female environment of St. Elizabeth's allowed her to extend her practices easily and support femaleness. She obviously considered the male point of view by virtue of the structure of the curriculum, but she critiqued it often; and she added the value of femaleness to her examples. The presence of young men might have created more tensions and debates about point of view and whether or not her comments and those of the young women would be considered "male-bashing." Thus, the absence of young men at St. Elizabeth's allowed her to engage her students in an open critique of male privilege.

These three accomplished teachers, specializing in different subject matter and operating in different school cultures, all communicated notions about what it means to be male and female in our schools. Charlene Wilson wanted to provide young women with the same opportunities for intellectual engagement that she had offered young men in the past – a goal that proved more difficult than she had anticipated. Brock Bronson wanted to improve his capacity to instill in all students a passion for mathematics, and in doing so welcomed young women especially. Nancy North felt the freedom to cast a conscientiously feminist lens on her study of history. All three teachers provided us rich data, helping us to be more thoughtful about the intended and the unintended gender consequences of classroom interactions and discourse.

4   Gendered Cultures and Students' Lives

Walking through the hallways at Xavier, St. Elizabeth's, and Grove made us keenly aware of the contrasts among the three schools, each with its own characteristic aura. Along with the variations one would find within any American high school – variations in tone, energy, formality, and informality – palpable differences in the tenor of each school emerged as we talked with students and faculty and watched how students interacted in classrooms and in hallways. At each school we saw different norms for behavior, for dress, for formal and informal student exchanges, and for exchanges between students and their teachers and administrators. In short, these schools differed in characteristics typically referred to as manifestations of the "culture" of an organization (Morgan, 1986). Edgar Schein (1985) described the term culture in organizations as: observed behavioral regularities, norms, dominant values espoused, philosophy, rules of the game, and feeling or climate (p. 6).

Environmental metaphors help to describe culture: organizational *climate*, negotiating varied *terrain*, capturing a unique *environment*. Each metaphor reveals the complex, subtle, and interdependent nature of the characteristics of culture in a school organization. Certain attributes further describe culture: artifacts (e.g., mascots, physical arrangements of classrooms or hallways, clothing styles, language, ceremonies), articulated beliefs (e.g., mission statements, publications), values as espoused ideals (what people say they value), and assumptions, which are tacit beliefs, implied through behavior, that may or may not be congruent with articulated values. To look at school culture, then, is to look at the overt and subtle messages that consciously, subconsciously, and unconsciously guide the making of policy and influence individuals' behavior. More accurately, we might say that an organization has many cultures, or subcultures, and individuals usually do not participate in all of the subcultures that exist (Martin, 1992).

To understand organizational behavior, we must understand how individuals perceive the cultural environment and how they are influenced by it. Individuals may participate in many subcultural environments at once and share in the creation of articulated and tacit assumptions, values, meanings, and messages that reflect the perception of those environments.

We consider schools "gendered cultures," although we do not suggest any intended malevolence or conscious conspiracy to shortchange females or males. Individual teachers and administrators typically want to help female and male students achieve their highest potential. Nonetheless, institutions, through their policies and practices and through their collective understandings about what constitutes teaching and learning, unconsciously communicate normative behavior about gender (Zanders, 1993).

In this chapter, we examine students and their experiences in our three high schools with a particular focus on the young women at Xavier during its first year of coeducation. During the time we studied these schools, each had a particular identity derived from its role in the coeducation decision – gender considerations were at the forefront. Xavier had spent several years planning for the admission of young women; St. Elizabeth's, after carefully considering concerns for its future, had reaffirmed its commitment to be an all-female school; and Grove High School had adopted strategies to attract males to a previously all-female high school. All three had something to prove: at Xavier, the female students could be successfully integrated into the once all-male school; at St. Elizabeth's, that there remained not only a need, but a market for female single-sex education; and at Grove, that the school could survive or, better yet, thrive as a coeducational school, despite increased competition. Students at all three schools well understood these circumstances.

Methodology

Over the course of two years, we gathered information from students about their high schools through written surveys, structured interviews, and student focus groups. We asked questions about the six different areas: academics, athletics and extra-curricular activities, peer social relationships, classroom dynamics, leadership, and community.

Survey Data

At Xavier, students responded to a series of written statements about their school using a 5-point scale Likert survey (from "I mostly disagree" to "I mostly agree"). During the year immediately prior to the coeducation transition, male students in the 9th, 10th, and 11th grades responded. We gave a similar survey after the first year of coeducation to all returning males, asking about their experiences with coeducation. We asked females questions about their experience during the transition year. Out of a population of 480 male students at freshmen through junior levels, 255 completed the first-year survey. Out of 550 males at the freshmen through senior levels,

481 completed the second-year survey. And 178 females, 9th through 12th grade, completed the second-year survey about their experience during the transition year.

Structured Interviews

We interviewed fifteen young women across all grades prior to their entry into Xavier Preparatory. Seven in-coming students were from public schools and eight came from other Catholic schools, including three transfers from St. Elizabeth's, two transfers from Grove, and three entering 9th graders from local Catholic grade schools. Most young women indicated that they chose Xavier because their parents wanted them to attend, and they had friends or brothers who had attended. A third group reported choosing Xavier because of its excellence in academics and athletics. Overall, the young women who entered Xavier during the transition year expected to be welcomed, although they also anticipated difficulties. Some had heard that young men did not want young women to enter Xavier; several predicted the first few months of coeducation would be the hardest, but then things would work out. They maintained generally hopeful expectations. One young woman expressed the sentiments of her female peers: "Once they get used to us, they'll be really glad to have us."

Focus Groups

We formed four student focus groups across the three sites. At Xavier and St. Elizabeth's, pairs of our research team met monthly with eight to ten young women from multiple grade levels to talk about particular topics we introduced and to find out how students viewed their school as well as their relationships with peers and teachers. At Grove, two of us met once with the student body officers (all seniors and all women), who were in the last all-female class to graduate from the high school. One of us was joined by a male researcher to meet twice with six young men at Xavier, students returning after the change to coeducation, to discuss their perceptions of the school.

Student Predictions of Change: Survey Results

Prior to coeducation, 98 percent of Xavier males predicted the school would change when young women entered. After coeducation 99 percent of returning students confirmed that the school was different and the school atmosphere had changed. What did the young men expect? Prior to coeducation, males predicted young women would distract them, would increase competition for grades, that young men would "show off," and that the school would lose its sense of community. Following the first year of coeducation, returning male students responded that indeed, some things had changed. Young men indicated that the atmosphere was different, but they tended not to make a value judgment. "Xavier is extremely different from last year, but that does not necessarily mean it is better or worse." Many males reported that the increase in school size had a greater effect than the entrance of young women. One male student explained: "Girls have made the school bigger and this has made Xavier lose its sense of tight community. It's still a community, but it's not the same Xavier as it was last year." Several young men viewed the arrival of young women favorably: "Like it or not, this is the real world. The integration of women into our school has been a necessary and positive experience. People may not realize this, or opt not to recognize its importance; it is their loss."

Students predicted that Xavier would change with coeducation, and many of their predictions were confirmed during the transition year. Although some young men lamented the loss of community as they had known it, they suggested the increased school size was just as responsible for changes as was the advent of young women.

Students Reflect on Their Schools: Focus Group Data

The data collected during focus groups reinforce a number of ideas that surfaced elsewhere in the study. We have chosen to summarize the results here because of the data's richness and its capacity to illuminate cross-site similarities and differences. Specifically, we look now at how students in each school viewed each of the following:

1 academics,
2 athletics and extra-curricular activities,
3 peer social relationships,
4 classroom dynamics,
5 student leadership, and
6 the school community.

Academics

The academic missions of all three schools were markedly similar; each purported a desire to develop students' intellectual, physical, social, and spiritual characteristics. Each emphasized its commitment to Catholic education, and each stressed the importance of serving others with a social justice agenda. The three schools, however, each committed behaviorally to these ideals to varying degrees and thus their students experienced different and sometimes conflicting messages about priorities, possibilities, and individual potential – all of which the high school students factored into their daily decisions and their interpretations of their schools' gendered cultures.

Academics at Xavier

People at Xavier expressed pride in the school's academic mission, clearly articulated in the literature and by the staff. The school prepares its students to attend a four-year college. It boasts a highly structured traditional curriculum guided by Ignatian pedagogy, small classes, and teachers who demand a great deal from their students. Female students were attracted to Xavier's high academic standards. One student explained: "We knew I was going here ever since Xavier was talking about going coed. Both of my brothers went here. My family wanted me to go here. It was the accepted thing. Xavier is strong academically. It's well known." Another student said: "I came to Xavier mainly for the academics. At Xavier I like the facilities, the academics are good. The public schools are not doing so good (sic)."

Students emphasized that being a solid Xavier student gave a competitive edge when applying to a good college. Graduates regularly attend high-ranking colleges and universities in the Midwest and East such as Georgetown, Notre Dame, Brown, and William and Mary, or in the West coast such as University of San Diego, Stanford, and Santa Clara. Parents and school personnel communicated high expectations for academic performance. Many students had hopes for athletic or academic scholarships. Female and male students cited these high expectations and recognized their privileged status. As one female student said, "We are well off; our parents are sending us here." Students also reported the pressure for academic achievement because of Xavier's high status and the substantial tuition costs.

> I need to keep my grades up. I don't have to go to West Point or the Naval Academy or whatever, I just don't want to end up at a community college. With my parents having paid for me to come here, it's kind of like I should do much better than that.

With the arrival of young women at Xavier, neither the academic mission nor the academic curriculum changed. The teachers and administrators saw no need to revise the academic program with the introduction of young women. The program had produced male scholars who were successful in elite university programs; its mission was to provide the same opportunities for young women. The concept of the "primacy of the male" influenced the academic programs at Xavier; males provided the norm and females were expected to fit the same normative pattern. And females did, by and large, accept the normative patterns for academic achievement and success. They expected to be academically challenged and they were.

In the female focus groups we heard young women talk about "being scared" and "not ready" for college and experiencing "so much pressure" with the expectation that they maintain a high grade point average at Xavier. Perhaps they had to demonstrate they were up to the task and as serious about pursuing a profession as were their male peers and siblings. Today's society expects most young women to develop career goals. All young women in the focus groups at Xavier expected to have a career and a family. Young women at St. Elizabeth's and at Grove treated these pressures about the simultaneous expectations of career and family somewhat differently.

Academics at St. Elizabeth's

The school letterhead reads "education uniquely focused on young women." A banner across the school entrance hanging next to two national Exemplary School Awards also bears the message: "130 Years of Making a Difference." The young women from St. Elizabeth's shared with Xavier's young women a commitment to academic excellence. Their comments included: "I decided to come to St. Elizabeth's when I was in the 5th grade because my sister went here and really liked it" and "I chose it because of its strong academic reputation."

Young women at St. Elizabeth's had high expectations of going to good colleges, similar to the colleges named by Xavier students. But discernible differences also existed. St. Elizabeth's women exhibited career inclinations, but wanted to "do what interests me." One young woman said, "I don't want to be something I don't enjoy ... something that wouldn't let me expand." Although they clearly worked hard and cared about getting good grades so they could get into a good college, the St. Elizabeth's young women didn't talk about career pressure and stress in the same way that several Xavier young women and men did. They cherished the independence they pictured in the future. They looked forward to making their own choices and felt prepared to be more "on my own." Many of the young women told us, "I can do anything."

Academics at Grove

Grove High School was working toward clarifying its academic mission at the time of our study. While always considered strong academically, prior to the coeducation transition, Grove did not share the elite college-preparatory reputations of the other two high schools. Most Grove graduates intended to continue their education in college, but, unlike their counterparts at Xavier and St. Elizabeth's, most would attend local colleges and universities. For example, all of the Grove student focus group participants planned to attend college – most within the state.

However, Grove's pressure for academic achievement was different from the other schools. On the one hand, the school felt the need to be academically competitive with Xavier and St. Elizabeth's. On the other hand, administrators found that, at least initially, the young men admitted were not of the same academic caliber as their female peers. The senior women in our focus group noted this differential treatment for males and females.

They took issue with the ways they perceived the administration had courted boys to attend Grove and applied different standards for admission; they believed the boys, as a group, met lower academic standards for admission. "They let guys in who got kicked out of public schools," several seniors reported. Indeed, at a faculty focus group meeting, Grove faculty acknowledged that the school had used different academic standards to admit young men in order to "get a critical mass" – although this was not public knowledge. All agreed that Grove needed to rethink its admission policies and practices.

We noted the contrast between modifying academic standards at Grove and the situation at Xavier. Whereas Xavier made the decision to include young women in the standard curriculum developed for young men, Grove changed the standards as young men entered. At Xavier, what was good for boys was seen as good for girls. High academic standards were an expectation at Xavier and cited as an important recruitment message during the transition to coeducation. At Grove, a more pragmatic approach was taken. In contrast to Xavier, Grove's academic standards were lowered to attract males to the school and to establish a coeducational student body. The unspoken assumption of the primacy of the male left the curriculum and admission standards essentially unchanged at Xavier, whereas at Grove admission standards were diminished to accommodate less qualified male students. Interestingly, however, from the students' perspective at both Grove and Xavier, those who had participated previously in a single-sex environment blamed the entrance of the members of the other sex for reducing standards.

Athletics and Extra-curricular Activities

Respected for its academic quality, Xavier also has a strong reputation for athletics, regularly sending teams to the state championship play-offs, especially for football and soccer. Indeed, Xavier athletics are so strong that it traditionally plays at the highest conference level with much larger schools. Xavier expects students to be "well rounded" and to "have a balance" between sports and academics. Most young women who entered Xavier fit this profile; they were academically oriented and athletically talented. The faculty at Xavier were committed to providing equal opportunities in athletics for females. In fact, major changes at Xavier had to do with athletics; their new buildings included a new gym and new locker room for females, and they created women's teams in each area (volleyball replacing football) to provide equal sports options. Some young men were impressed by the positive contributions young women made to athletics at Xavier. One student noted that "they established a lot of women's sports; I was impressed. They did a great job." Another pointed out that "all sports have been successful, the (women's) soccer team is dominating." Indeed, since the time our data were collected, several women's teams have excelled at state and regional levels. In 1998 Xavier women's soccer team won the state championship five times out of its six years of existence.

Both males and females at Xavier experienced strong pressure to participate in athletics; athletic competition was not as strong at St. Elizabeth's nor at Grove. While some Xavier young women believed that "everyone is respected for what they do," they recognized pressure to participate in sports. They saw getting on a team as "very competitive." Some female students regarded competition as valuable and looked forward to the opportunity. Other young women chose not to participate. A female freshman reported that because Xavier had recruited so many good women for soccer and she didn't believe she was that good, she decided not to try out. Alternatively, the truly athletically oriented young women at Xavier talked about how important it was to participate in sports, and though they acknowledged the competitive nature of sports at Xavier, "the emphasis is on the team." They valued the high quality of team spirit and shared responsibility for success. A female freshman said: "I feel better around those (well-rounded) people. When I'm with them, I feel like I'm headed for success because they're headed for success." Again, as with Xavier academics, male athletes provided the normative standard and most females embraced it.

A different story, however, unfolded at Grove. Young women noted a negative difference in sports since boys entered the high school. School spirit had waned for the athletic teams, although the number of sports and kinds of sports offered had increased. "Sports were a real source of pride for the school, and now the guys come in and it's hard when you're going to a game every night to have much spirit." Assemblies didn't seem as "peppy" and students "don't really get into the spirit of assemblies like we used to." The senior girls believed the boys had diminished Grove school spirit by labeling as "uncool" certain spirit rally activities that had become traditional and considered fun, such as putting on skits, dressing in costume, and lip-synching.

Cheerleading, an activity primarily designated as "female" in the high schools of the United States, took an interesting turn at Xavier. Some young men expressed anger that young women became dominant on the cheerleading squad; of fifteen cheerleaders only two or three were boys. In prior years, the male cheerleaders were a rag-tag informal group that sometimes was an embarrassment to the school staff. With the addition of girls, a professional coach was hired and the cheerleading squad became polished with practiced routines and uniforms. The new norms for cheerleaders led to some instances of hostility from male students. A female student told us: "There were instances when the (cheerleading) squad got picked on. The first two weeks were harsh. Seniors used to get the first row (of seating), but there was competition between the senior class and the cheerleaders."

Interestingly, after its rocky introduction, cheerleading soon took on the attributes and expectations of an important sport at Xavier. In the Xavier winning tradition, the cheerleading squad entered and won state and regional championships in only its second year of competition.

While Xavier students valued winning teams, extra-curricular participation also included drama, band, or one of many clubs. Female and male students at Xavier told us the school honors different student interests, although they considered extra-curricular involvement of some kind essential. "There's very rarely someone who doesn't belong to something."

To St. Elizabeth's students, the importance of becoming engaged in extra-curricular activities was as a way to meet people, to have a sense of belonging, to serve as "a stress reducer," or to improve one's chances of getting into college. They were less interested in being competitive and preferred "non-tryout activities" where everyone who wished to participate could. St. Elizabeth's drama productions, model United Nations, and service clubs had especially high participation.

All three schools supported high levels of student involvement in athletics and other extra-curricular activities as a means of students becoming well-rounded citizens, preparing for college, expressing the values of community service, and participating fully in high school. Although each school engaged students differently, they had in common their selective Catholic school culture which emphasizes student engagement. Several different studies point out that Catholic school culture promotes high student involvement; such engagement supports the norms, values, and expectations for a cohesive culture with high expectations for student performance (Bryk et al., 1993; NCEA, 1985; Riordon, 1990).

Peer Social Relations

Although peer relationships are of utmost importance to all adolescents, some significant sex differences in friendship patterns exist. For females, adolescent friendships tend to serve the purposes of intimacy, commitment, and loyalty; for males, friendships more often serve the purposes of achievement, competitive advantage, and leadership (Hallinen, 1981). The students we studied expected to find differences in peer social relationships in single-sex and coeducational schools and they did. In this section, we discuss three issues about peer relationships most often raised by students: (1) cross-sex relationships, (2) cliques, and (3) issues of belonging.

Cross-sex relationships

Young men at Xavier, and young women at Grove and St. Elizabeth's, predicted the biggest change resulting from the coeducation decision would be in cross-sex relationships. Females at Grove High School believed that they would be intimidated by young men in the classroom, that males would be disruptive and interfere with learning and that the young women would have to pay more attention to their looks and dress. Males at Xavier also mentioned needing to pay more attention to their appearance. In addition, they believed that the presence of young women would increase classroom competition for grades, that male-to-male friendships might be jeopardized, and that males would pay more attention to their girlfriends than to their male friends. Regarding cross-sex relationships, one young woman at Xavier who had previously attended a public school noted that in public coeducational schools:

> There are so many more couples. Everyone has a boyfriend. I have a friend [going to public school next year] and she just feels that pressure, that if she doesn't have someone right now she's going to be below all the others.

The Xavier females who entered the upper grades during the first year of coeducation held a unique perspective, especially in comparison to those who entered as 9th graders. One junior woman expressed a common observation:

> I kind of envy this freshman group. They seem like they really are good friends with guys. It's cool because they seem really close and I'd like to do that.

Some young men at Xavier noted they were uncomfortable in the presence of girls, "Lots of guys aren't comfortable and don't have a lot of interaction with the girls." But they added they were learning how to act around girls. Both sexes believed that cross-sex romantic relationships would change same-sex friendships. A male student reported: "Friends will get a girlfriend and now they will have their girls in their life and the girls will take over more of their time."

Some Xavier young men said they liked it better when the girls were at St. Elizabeth's and Grove. Attending school at Xavier then was for "hanging out" with the guys and the evenings and weekends were for dating and spending time with girlfriends. Xavier males were reluctant to give up the "fellowship or camaraderie in the all-male classes" and were disturbed that "friendships could be affected by having a girl come between them." Indeed, even faculty expressed concern that male students would not easily share their emotional and vulnerable side with young women present, as they might have felt more comfortable doing when the school was all-male.

At St. Elizabeth's, students expressed appreciation for the perceived "freedom" in relations their single-sex environment afforded them. Several talked about "at first feeling deprived without boys," but over time, they "couldn't even imagine going to school with boys."

Presence of cliques

Xavier young men predicted females would form cliques that would jeopardize the easy, relaxed, inclusive male–male relationships they had previously enjoyed. They expected that women would exert their personal power, managing social relationships through "cliques" – small, impenetrable groups of students who socially exclude others. Although cliques had not formed to the degree predicted by males, females at Xavier confirmed that some cliques had formed, and furthermore, they were exclusionary. Examples of newly formed cliques included groups of students who had transferred from St. Elizabeth's, certain social class groupings, and some from particular middle schools.

A female Xavier freshman in the focus group impressed us with her sense of self-confidence and assertiveness. She pointed out that she had developed friendships purposefully with peers from many different groups. She described Xavier as "like the high schools you read about in books – sports, family feeling, spirit. You can be different here. You just need to find your own way to be different." She told us she had friends "all spread out all over throughout the freshman class. Everybody has their own circle of friends, but I have a few from each kind of circle." She tried to get them together by having them at a pajama party at her house, her party was a success but it did not get the young women together in school. "They're starting to get along better." A junior echoed this theme of developing friendship by telling of a shy girl whom she got to know well at the junior class encounter. "And now she talks all the time. I mean, she doesn't over talk, but she is not quiet."

School size did not appear to affect the perceived presence of student cliques. St. Elizabeth's was a much smaller school than Xavier, yet some described it as very "cliquey." Others felt "groupie" was a better description of St. Elizabeth's. Feelings of exclusion seemed to be less a problem at St. Elizabeth's because there was a strong cultural norm to recognize and honor the uniqueness of each young woman. Students talked about different circles of friends and that "there is a place for everyone." Students at all the schools, similar to most adolescents, worried about friendship and the problem of being an outsider. The students shared the common need for assurance of acceptance and a place within their school community.

Feelings of belonging

In Australia, Marsh et al. (1988) studied the effects on self-concept of a change from single-sex schools to coeducation. They concluded that changes in organizational reconfigurations pose unique challenges to young adolescents in self-concept and the sense of belonging but they noted no sex differences in self-concept.

Although we did not study self-concept directly, we noted differences in how the need for belonging played out at Xavier and St. Elizabeth's. At St. Elizabeth's, young women feared being "hurt" by being looked down upon, or considered stupid. They reflected on "fear of people not liking you; of being wrong," and "fear of people laughing at you," or of "boring everyone to death" by talking too much. As a freshman stated, "If you don't say things, then you won't have to risk things. You might not want to start your four years here with a bad reputation." Although St. Elizabeth's young women generally found and developed strong voices and self-confidence, and claimed to be able to speak out, being perceived as "wrong" or "stupid" was still an issue in the same-sex setting. They claimed, however, they would be less vocal in coeducational settings.

Xavier women felt concerned about their place in school; they wondered where they belonged among their peers. We heard about a student who "worries a lot about what people are thinking of her." Another student said: "I felt a lot of pressure to do volleyball. I wanted to try out for the play. I didn't want to do volleyball but a lot of my friends were and I didn't want to feel left out."

The change to coeducation at Xavier High School heightened student awareness of social relationships. Both students and teachers closely examined how young women would perform at Xavier and whether their presence would be a negative or positive factor on males. While male students who previously attended Xavier lamented the loss of the close camaraderie in an all-male school, they also talked of the benefits gained from having young women attend their school.

In conclusion, young men at Xavier thought the entrance of women would seriously affect the social relationships of the school culture. And they were correct. We also noted the strong sense of individual agency of the young women at both Xavier and St. Elizabeth's. The young women attending Xavier in the first year of coeducation stood out as athletic, bright, and socially adept, just like their young male counterparts. They knew what they wanted and were not afraid to pursue it; they fit in well with the Xavier culture. The young women at St. Elizabeth's expressed normal fears about being accepted and belonging, yet the culture of their school cultivated acceptance and understanding of uniqueness and of qualities varying from typical definitions of popularity. The senior women at Grove mourned the loss of comfortable and intimate female–female relationships as their social world transformed with the arrival of boys. They criticized their younger classmates, who "dressed for school" and "wore make-up" – all the while feeling powerless to impact the changes.

Classroom Group Dynamics

Students participating in focus groups had the most heightened awareness of sex bias and spoke the most vocally about their experiences in the classroom; males at Xavier and females at Grove believed teachers preferred and favored the other sex. They noted demeaning remarks or jokes made by teachers or other students, and both sexes believed the dynamics of the classroom had changed dramatically with the introduction of the other sex.

Relationships with teachers

Prior to coeducation at Xavier, 93 percent of the young men predicted teachers would teach differently; after coeducation, 88 percent of the returning young men believed teachers had changed their teaching. Primarily, they found teachers more sensitive about telling jokes or making comments that could be interpreted as demeaning or sexist, although they reported some teachers still persisted with such behaviors. Young women at Xavier also commented about remarks by teachers which were demeaning toward females; in contrast, young women at Grove High School made no mention of teachers making demeaning remarks regarding males.

With the doubling of the student body at Xavier, the teaching staff also doubled in size and included a large increase in the percentage of female teachers. Students noticed differences in their teachers, and mentioned anxieties communicated through comments from teachers and staff: A male student noted: "Teachers who have been here all their lives are just overwhelmed. They are getting so tired. There is so much stress now."

Male Xavier students noted some of the really "gruff" teachers had changed their tactics. For instance, the teacher who threw tennis balls to get the young men to pay attention stopped using that aggressive technique when females entered the classroom. Other teachers remained tough; as one student said, "Mr. X cares ... physical torment is to show he loves us." In contrast, students at Grove High School and at St. Elizabeth's gave no indications that any teacher engaged in the "gruff" behavior attributed to some male teachers at Xavier.

Both young men at Xavier and young women at Grove believed teachers paid more attention to the other sex. But teacher–student interaction data presented by researchers Myra and David Sadker (1994) and Deborah Tannen (1990) supported the females' perceptions; teachers call on boys more frequently, give them more time to respond and ask more probing questions of boys than of girls. Our Xavier classroom observation data corroborate these findings. We traced student and teacher talk in several classes. Some teachers consciously tried to be "fair" and call on students equally; even so, males received more attention and had more "talk time" than females. While "talk time" is important, also important is the kind of discourse that occurs in a classroom (Hiller, 1998). Our field notes recorded an unfortunate interaction involving a male algebra teacher and a female student at Xavier:

> Toward the end of the class period, students began filling out their registration forms for next year's classes. A female student approached the teacher and said she wanted to move to an accelerated math class. The teacher glanced at her and responded, "I don't think that is a good idea; your work is too sloppy." He then moved to a male who had been talking loudly to the entire class that he was going to take math "all four years" because it would look good on his college applications. The teacher smiled and told him that was a very good idea.
>
> (Beacom, 1994)

Field notes from this particular day also described the general negative and competitive tone of the class, and in this incident captured the belittling of the female student's intelligence while allowing a male student to disrupt the class and draw the teacher's attention toward himself. While there is no evidence to suggest that such exchanges were the norm, the event was a prototype of how sex biases, although often subtle, usually were obvious to the female students we interviewed.

Xavier males and Grove females believed the dynamics of their single-sex classrooms changed dramatically with the move to coeducation. In both schools, students claimed that teachers favored the other sex and perceived that the other sex "gets away with murder." And both sexes described behaviors that are consonant with stereotypes of male and female behavior. For instance, Xavier male students said: "Girls are argumentative in class." Another said, "A lot of girls are afraid of getting the wrong answer. A lot of them don't understand." Some young men complained that with the entrance of young women, the looser and more permissive all-male environment and their habit of "joking around with guys" had ended.

Grove senior women made observations similar to those of the Xavier men who were used to a single-sex setting. Coeducation changed the classroom, making certain informal ways of relating no longer appropriate. The young women from Grove reported that in the past, in their all-female classes,

> We used to talk about everything. We'd joke about family and boyfriends and stuff like that. Now we can't joke about anything because if you do the guys kinda take over the topic and go off in their own world.

And teachers:

> used to get mad if you didn't raise your hand. Now it's just like, don't

talk over people and don't interrupt them; if you're going to interrupt them, don't yell. Guys just blurt out, even if it's wrong; they'll just yell it out anyway.

Grove young women pointed to a general decline, in their view, in how people cared for each other at their school. A senior woman observed, "The rules that are respectful toward other people have become lax. It doesn't really matter anymore." Senior Grove females also articulated grievances about males entering their school, sharing several stories about the effects on teachers and classroom interactions in their newly coeducational classes.

> One class that's really different [with boys now] is the music class. The teachers are so sexist. They're like, "Oh, have the men come down and move this." We can't volunteer to do anything. The class is 3:1, girls to guys. [Asked whether the girls used to help move music stands they told us ...], Oh, yeah. She used to say, "Okay, can we get some strong people down here and [we would help]." Now it's just like, "Can we get some of these big guys? Let's have some men come down here." And it's just like, "Excuse me, it's not that heavy."

Some who had attended the adjacent St. Theresa Elementary School (which had converted to coeducation years before but never changed its name) confirmed this differential practice in early grade school:

> Even though the boys were like half our size, they were still short in eighth grade, and they were still asked to move stuff. It's the idea, "Boys are finally here; girls don't have to do anything." Almost all of us were brought up to be independent and to be able to do stuff like that, because obviously most of us are sitting here for that reason, so that we could be independent women. It's just disgusting.

Perturbed by the preference given to males in the music class, they felt equally annoyed by the opposite situation with their male coaches on the track team and in swimming.

> The guys sit there with their walkman while the girls move the high jump pits and everything. It's supposed to be the girls move them out, the guys take them in, but it ends up the girls take them out and the girls take them in.

And in swimming, the coach "never asks the guys to do anything. He always asks the girls to carry everything."

Young Xavier women, for the most part, complimented the teachers and the academic standards at Xavier. "Academically the school is very difficult, yet, at the same time, teachers truly want you to succeed and they will do what is necessary to help you reach your goals. The teachers are very dedicated and I appreciate them."

A few noted, however, that some teachers were not used to working with young women and that the curriculum was male-dominated: "Many teachers have not had the chance to teach girls and do not know how to associate with them. Some treat us as if we are equal to boys – we are different." "There is a need for teachers to realize even if there are four girls in a class they need to also speak to them, and about things they can be involved in, not just sports." The literature on girls' experiences of gender differences in classroom settings corroborates these feelings of being either ignored or treated the same as boys (Barba and Cardinale, 1991; Lockheed, 1985; Sadker and Sadker, 1994; Sadker et al., 1991; Streitmatter et al., 1996).

Keenly aware of changes in the way their former teachers acted in the classroom, both the Xavier young men and the Grove young women thought teachers had become more lax with the advent of coeducation. Both groups believed teachers favored the other sex, although our classroom observations showed that even in the most sex-equitable classrooms, boys talked more often than girls and generally controlled the nature and direction of the classroom discourse.

Students noticed changes in the enforcement of prior behavior policies and expressed concern about the lowering of standards, whether the school was now admitting young men (Grove) or young women (Xavier) as it became coeducational. Our data from interviews with a faculty focus group suggest that Grove High School did lower standards for admission, in an effort, according to senior class women, to increase enrollment for young men. And data suggest that social and behavioral norms changed. Female reports on classroom dynamics and student–teacher relationships revealed the presence of traditional sex-biased expectations.

Our study of teachers' perceptions at Xavier (Nagel et al., 1994) showed a majority of teachers believed that girls matched or exceeded the high academic standards of males. Xavier teachers admitted classroom dynamics and behavior standards had changed somewhat. Young men at Xavier may have interpreted a softening of the tone of the learning environment as a lowering of standards. Certainly, they had to share their learning environments with young women under new and different terms and any change could fuel the perception that the females received more attention. We, however, found no support for their claim.

Student Leadership

Most high schools want to develop student leadership and Catholic schools emphasize it even more (Bryk et al., 1993; Riordan, 1990). The three schools we studied emphasized leadership as a critical part of the educational mission. The history of societal leadership in the Western world, however, is steeped in the male prerogative, and the scholarly literature on leadership is primarily based on the study of those in positions of authority in industry and in the military – and thus, primarily men. A growing body of literature using females as subjects for studies on leadership fuels a current debate about whether or not females and males lead differently; data support similarities and differences (Dunlap and Schmuck, 1995).

When asked to think of leaders, people, both females and males, usually think of men – a stereotype exhibited in the two coeducational schools we studied. The leader-as-male stereotype surfaced at Grove where male students in the formerly all-female school took over all the student body officer positions for a number of years – all except the position of secretary. At Xavier, females won no student body officer positions except secretary during the first five years of coeducation. Student leadership at St. Elizabeth's obviously provided a counterexample.

The characteristics of leading

We asked students in focus groups at all three schools to identify the qualities of leaders in their school and to describe the characteristics of leaders in general. Clear differences emerged in the ways young men and young women constructed the concept of leadership and identified the basis of leadership.

At Xavier, five young women participated in the female focus group on leaders and leadership; six young men participated in an all-male session on the subject. At St. Elizabeth's, ten young women attended the leadership session. We tape recorded and transcribed all sessions. From each transcription, we listed all the different attributes of leaders generated during the discussion. Next, we examined all three lists and grouped similar descriptions together, ending up with seven attribute categories. The statements reflect the variability among leaders and diverse styles of leadership (see Table 4.1). It is notable that young women at both schools generated more characteristics in more categories than did Xavier's young men. We cannot attribute this to differences in the number of focus group participants since Xavier's young women – the smallest group – generated the most characteristics overall and in all categories.

Table 4.1 indicates that young women had a broad view of leadership and a deep understanding of what it means to lead. They told us that leaders possess skills such as how to run an effective meeting and when to take charge, and can work well with others. They also generated a long list of personality traits, including many specific comments about courage, confidence, and personal style – "acts like a leader." Young men said nothing about process skills, and only mentioned personality twice: once to say a leader might be a "natural" one because of personality and a second time to note that leaders are "spirited." While both young women's groups talked about spirited, energetic, and outgoing personalities among leaders, both also talked of "silent leaders" with a special "presence" and an ability to "bring people in one at a time." Many of the ideas the young women expressed had to do with relationships between leaders and followers, consistent with the literature indicating females think more "relationally" than do males (Belenky et al., 1986; Felker, 1993; Lyons et al., 1990; Rosener, 1990).

The young women's more elaborate discourse included many examples of what leadership and leaders look like. The discourse among Xavier's young men focused mainly on assigned or elected leadership positions or seniority. For example, "the leaders are the seniors" because they are older and more mature. Within the five categories related more to character, personality, and interpersonal skills, Xavier young men generated only five ideas, with no mention of intelligence or of process skills, and nothing suggesting a place for courage, confidence, or assertiveness. Many female students openly rejected a positional or authority-based view of leadership. A St. Elizabeth's student asserted, "*Leadership* is more person-based. *Authority* is more power based." Another added, "I think authority is a different kind of leadership, a sort of forced leadership."

Students in all three groups talked about whether official school officers, members of the Association of Student Bodies (ASB), are leaders. Most males, and many young women at Xavier, said ASB officers are student leaders. St. Elizabeth's students, on the other hand, rejected the idea that an ASB position automatically defined a person as a leader. One female remarked that "ASB officers may have authority to make decisions but authority is given to you. Leadership is earned."

It is valuable to note that St. Elizabeth's has a collaborative form of student government in contrast to the traditional, hierarchical form of student government at Grove and Xavier. Five students at St. Elizabeth's are elected to serve as an "Association of Student Bodies Cabinet" and use a shared governance model to manage the ASB affairs and concerns in the school. Focus group comparisons between the schools indicate a strong sense of "ownership," "the ability to make change," and "powerfulness" at St. Elizabeth's. In contrast, at Xavier there was less of a perception of "ownership" and more of an acceptance of "buying into" the discipline and culture of the school because "what I will become is special." A perception of powerlessness is tolerated at Xavier because the end product, "being an Xavier graduate," is highly desired by the students and their parents.

Distinctions in how students understood leadership point to the significant social learning that occurs through the gendered cultures of the environment. Some learning about leadership may occur through the official curriculum, but for the most part, students develop their conceptions of leaders and leadership through messages and models in the larger society, the cumulative experiences in a school culture, and their informal relationships with staff and one another.

Table 4.1 *Student Responses to the Questions: What is leadership, and who are the leaders in your school/class?*

Attribute Categories	Females At St. Elizabeth's (n=10)	Females At Xavier (n = 5)	Males At Xavier (n = 6)
Position	Student council members, people who urge others to do the right thing, people who take or are assigned leadership positions. (Added, teachers/administrators should not assign student leadership positions.) Not always part of ASB.	ASB officers, those whom a teacher or administrator assigns to organize or lead.	ASB officers, those whom a teacher or administrator assigns to organize or lead.
Age /Maturity	Younger people look up to seniors, being a leader is being older. Older students know more, e.g., about classes, sports, drama, and so on.	Seniors. Juniors. Age. The leaders are seniors. Freshmen and sophomores don't have leaders, but upperclassmen do. Juniors and seniors all seem like leaders. Girls who transfer to Xavier have to be leaders. More girls are leaders at a younger age – girls mature earlier. The most outspoken guy is the leader.	People follow after them.
Being A Role Model	Someone people admire. Someone who sets an example. In sports, older, more capable students who lead practices, tell people what to do, but are nice and supportive. Athletes; others look up to them.	Someone you respect, admire, look up to, who you'd like to be like, who sets an example for others, who does things first – a trend-setter, who takes a role as leader in, e.g., a sport or drama because s/he is more capable. Athletes; others look up to them.	Someone who takes a role as leader in, e.g., sports or drama because s/he is more capable and others look up to the person.
Intelligence	Knowledgeable about what s/he is leading.	On the honor roll. Knows everything. Is smart.	Nothing said in this category.
Personality	Appealing, outgoing. Leaders have courage to talk, stand up for what they believe, give unpopular opinions, are willing to be a minority, confident, aggressive, assertive, willing to question the teacher, to speak their mind, outspoken. Some are silent leaders; they bring people in one at a time.	Not self-conscious, having spirit, welcoming, not self-absorbed, energetic caring, understanding of others' views. They do things that make others want to follow, have a desire to lead. Better leaders like what they do. They have courage, are not afraid to talk in class, talk a lot, able to talk in front of others, not shy. Some are silent leaders; it's the way they hold themselves and do things, their presence.	Spirited. Some are natural leaders because of personality. Note: nothing about courage or confidence, or about silent leaders.
Process Skills	Leaders start conversations and are responsible for getting things done.	Leaders take charge; take over and get things done. They make the right decisions. They keep group discussions on the topic; keep others from fooling around in class.	Nothing said in this category.
Works With And Respects Others	Nothing said in this category.	Good people who get along, listen, but keep their own ideas. They guide others but don't restrict them. They accept people for who they are, take others' ideas and incorporate them with their own. They help other students, help people, take responsibility for the group and do things so others won't get hurt.	Nice to everyone. They help other students, help other people.

The School Community

Each school we studied is a strong community. Indeed, these Catholic schools were formed around the concept of cohesive community. There is a clear, explicitly stated belief among faculty, administrators, staff, students, and parents that a "sense of community" is what sets their schools apart from others, most notably public high schools. We had a similar sense when visiting each of these schools; we could see and feel the quality of a community united. All members were bound together in their joint efforts, traditions, myths, and symbols. When it is strong and cohesive, community is palpable in a school.

Bryk et al.'s (1993) study of Catholic schools paid attention to the idea of "community," defined as "membership in a set of traditions and mores that reflect the group's purpose" (p. 128). They argued that a voluntary community, where students and parents must deliberately choose to participate (unlike public schools, which must take anyone who comes to their door), has greater power to build students' character and can lead to greater academic achievement. We agree. In schools that are voluntary communities, students by and large share the norms of the school or they leave. Paying school tuition tends to confirm students as members in a peer group that mirrors its values. Although all schools made an effort to recruit minority students and offer scholarships to less economically privileged youth, most students in all three schools came from families with some degree of economic and educational privilege. Among the schools, St. Elizabeth's best succeeded in bringing together the most diverse collection of students.

The presence or absence of the other sex made a difference in the way students experienced the community of their school. Students saw school community change with the introduction of the other sex; for instance, a Xavier male commented, "It is still a community but it isn't the same Xavier as it was last year." And a Grove female explained, "I came here because it was an all-female environment and because it was small. It's all changed now."

Senior young women at Grove perceived they were treated as second class citizens upon the admission of young men. They pointed out the behavior of younger women in the coed grades has "changed and they're giggly now"; and appearance had become important. "All they care about is what they're wearing." They also noted how males had become more dominant. "Guys seem to dominate meetings." Student government was another area of frustration. The Grove young women reported that "all class presidents for the coming year are boys" and "all student body officers are boys except for the secretary." They saw their status displaced as the administration and faculty focused on meeting the needs of males. One student pointed to a new brochure representing the school:

It just has guys in there. I mean, tons of guys, and where are the girls?

> For sports they had a picture of guys running track and guys' basket-ball, and then in the music group there should have been tons of girls, but the focus was on the guys. The funny thing is when the brochure was made there were only about 20 guys in the whole school, so all the same boys you saw over and over again.

The Grove seniors felt a loss of school spirit and the close bonding among students. They told us how the administration changed school traditions when males entered. For instance, students were no longer allowed to have initiation rituals for freshmen. The young women thought the administration had changed this policy because "they were afraid that with the guys here, the guys might take advantage of that or something." And they most strongly objected to the change in the school's name; whereas the school previously had been named after St. Theresa, the administration changed it to a less feminine name. "That was the most ridiculous thing in the world, changing the name so that it was less feminine so the boys would come here. That's what we were told, the reason they changed the name." And they wisely pointed out, "Xavier didn't change their name" to attract females.

While there was some difficulty at Xavier in establishing their coeducational community, the female students did not present the same degree of resentment:

> There is a little tension in the air between the boys and girls. The junior class boys, especially, don't like us, but hopefully that will soon change. There's no reason not to accept us. I mean, we're just a different gender.

The junior male class struggled the most with coeducation. Young women constituted only a small portion of the class and most of the young men had already spent two years in an all-male setting. Those males were the least comfortable and the most critical about the presence of young women. The senior class included only six young women, so senior males still spent most of their time within the company of males.

Despite some negative feelings among some Xavier males, women entering Xavier commented on the strong sense of community and how well accepted they felt. The Xavier female students frequently talked about an emphasis on "unity" and community; "They want you to know everyone in the class"; "They even have a day-long freshman retreat to promote unity and get to know each other." One young woman spoke about the strength of community feeling. "At Xavier they talk about you as though you're going to be a senior; they expect you to be here all four years." A sophomore admitted she was "kind of jealous of the freshmen who get to start out here [and] of the boys who have been here. They have their traditions and inside jokes that I don't understand."

A female Xavier freshman agreed her class had an advantage because of an equal number of young men and young women, unlike the other classes where boys were in the majority. Nonetheless, the general feeling was that teachers, administrators, and most of the boys were treating the girls fairly and appropriately: "I thought the boys would be really rude to the girls. I'm surprised; they're not." From another, we heard, "The teachers are good at including girls; they are not favoring girls. They are not being too lenient."

With the introduction of coeducation, both Xavier and Grove increased the size of their school. At Grove, the incoming freshmen class equaled twice the size of the graduating senior class, whereas at Xavier, the size of the entire school doubled. Everyone – staff, faculty, and students – considered the size of the school to be an important factor in the changing sense of community. Young men at Xavier noted this change: "That's the biggest loss this year. This is a huge school. I remember by last year second semester, I knew the whole school. Now I only know some of the freshmen."

At St. Elizabeth's, the decision to remain single-sex had a positive effect on its sense of community; the school reaffirmed its mission and proceeded to reinforce its norms about being a safe haven for young women. But this affirmative position was tenuous initially because many faculty members were worried the school would lose too many students once Xavier accepted females.

Similar to Xavier's and Grove's students, St. Elizabeth's young women expressed a strong sense of community. They were attracted by the small size, by the ability to recognize everybody, and to get to know people well, by the "laid back and comfortable atmosphere" and by "having people who care about you for who you are, not how you look."

Young women at St. Elizabeth's valued being in an all-female environment where they could avoid "distractions" and "discipline problems" created by young men:

> I visited [another] coed Catholic high school, but was really turned off. Guys took over most of the conversations in the classroom with the teachers; there were a lot of disciplinary problems with them and that was distracting.

> I used to be convinced that students at St. Elizabeth's were really deprived – didn't have cheerleaders or cute boys. I would look at friends going to other schools who would hang out with boys during breaks and I thought that was so cool. But now I can't even imagine going to school with boys.

The presence or absence of the other sex influenced the way students regarded their school community. The communities in both Xavier and Grove changed considerably with the introduction of the other sex.

Gendered Cultures

An all-female classroom and an all-female school are very different from an all-male classroom or an all-male school, and each of these stands in contrast with coeducational settings (Arnot, 1982; Felker, 1993). The very condition of being single-sex or coeducational results in different interaction patterns, forms of discourse, and sense of self. As the self is generated through the reflected appraisals of others, females especially have a different reflected self in an all-female setting than when males are present. Boys have "the privilege of learning in an environment that reflects back to them, through lessons, texts, exams and discussions, the images and knowledge of their own male culture" (Gosetti, 1995, p. 52). Girls, on the other hand, when in the same environment, see little reflection of their lives or their experiences (Style, 1988).

Each school we studied is academically sound, has sensitive and caring staff, boasts students who generally treat one another with respect, and is committed to students' learning about public service. Our data demonstrated that young women faced experiences in the all-female school unlike those in the coeducation school. In the coeducation setting femaleness was unrecognized and, in the case of one of the coeducational schools, even devalued, whereas in the all-female culture it was not only recognized, but revered.

We looked at how gender is communicated through aspects of school culture. We maintain two points about how the schools we studied are gendered:

1   The concept of male primacy affects school practice and policy; male students provide the standard norm and female students are the deviant "other."
2   The value of femaleness is higher in all-female schools than in coeducational settings, and females in single-sex settings develop stronger feelings of individual efficacy and power than in coeducational settings.

Primacy of the Male

Primacy of males means that the standard male norm is predominant; to be female is to be the "other," even to be deviant (Maher and Tetreault, 1994). Because maleness is highly valued, those who accept male primacy presume that what is good for boys is also good for girls. Xavier faculty members did not change the academic or the extra-curricular programs when females entered the school because they believed they already had the best curriculum and because they valued fairness and equity for all students. They sought to present young women with the same highly valued curriculum that they had been offering young men. Athletics also was important and Xavier planned and implemented an equally impressive athletic program for young women as a means of providing access for all students. The decision to offer the same valued resources for female students as for males did have an effect on Xavier males' experience at school. For instance, the men's athletic coaches complained that their potential pool of athletic talent would drop because teams would be smaller, a negative consequence for a select school in a highly competitive urban community.

Yet as males entered Grove High School, many changes occurred in the academic programs, curriculum, and extra-curricular offerings. As a school originally designed for girls, Grove was *not* good enough for boys. Although the coed transition began with the admission of boys to the freshmen class only, the school adopted a full, varsity-level basketball program from the start and hired a well-known coach with a history of success. The girls noticed this sudden and starkly contrasted commitment to sports excellence for boys.

So too, the emphasis on athletic excellence at Xavier affected St. Elizabeth's. St. Elizabeth's lost sophomore, junior, and senior athletes as transfers to Xavier. St. Elizabeth's braced for the reality that Xavier would hire strong coaches and its athletically oriented students might leave to play at a higher level of competition.

One incident at Xavier especially illustrates the deeply embedded assumption of a male-normative standard. During the first year of coeducation, a male student editor wrote an editorial in the Xavier school newspaper, which was read and approved by the female student assistant editor. The article described how girls had changed things at Xavier: teachers were more lax and the standards were falling. The editor attributed this decline in school standards to the presence of young women. The male principal called the two students to his office to discuss the article. He asked for data, but they had none. They both defended the article's premise on their personal impressions. The principal then raised the question, "Would you have written this article about African American students at our school?" Both said they wouldn't because it would be racist. "Then," he asked, "how can you write such an article about young women?" We are not surprised by the students' position, but it is poignant that an intelligent, aware, and capable young woman, who entered Xavier at a time of heightened consciousness about gender, would participate in the devaluation of females. Individual females, like members of other devalued groups, do not want to be devalued and will see themselves as an "exception" to their group, thus they deny there is discrimination against them (Crosby, 1984). They exhibit the standards of the predominant group (male) and may resent other females, or exhibit behaviors of self-hatred. Most female students and female faculty at Xavier unquestionably adopted the male standard. We suspect that the sexism of this editorial incident would not go unnoticed among the senior women at Grove High School or the young women at St. Elizabeth's. The senior women at Grove, who had only experienced being in an all-female setting, now had the experience of becoming "the other," and the female students at St. Elizabeth's (at least in Nancy North's class) were well versed in sexist behavior and practice.

One avowed purpose of Xavier's coeducational transition was to extend their curriculum of "leadership for service" to young women. It did not alter its curriculum, it did not change its focus; Xavier merely extended its existing offerings to females. Xavier adopted a "same is equal" policy. Some young women, however, raised issues about femaleness that had not been previously raised at Xavier. Descendants of post-Title IX reform, they did not behave submissively nor merely accept male primacy: "In religion classes when they talk about God they use 'He' but they're okay when girls bring up the question 'what if God is a she?' "

Grove gives the clearest example of male primacy beginning with the symbolic act of changing the school name to make it sound less "female." Grove leadership sought to create a different culture, more appealing to young men, assuming what was good for girls was not also good for boys. The young men, though a minority, changed the culture of Grove, significantly affecting freshmen initiations, assemblies, admissions, teacher interactions, peer relationships, and student-elected government.

Sense of Efficacy

The concept of self-efficacy helps explain the varied experiences of young women in the three schools. Efficacy refers to power and agency, important constructs in understanding relationships within a culture. Bandura (1982) described *self-efficacy* as a cognitive mechanism that regulates behavior. Bandura emphasized that perceived self-efficacy is a situation-specific determinant of behavior, not a global personality trait, and he stressed that the study of self-efficacy must include contextual influences. According to Ashton and Webb (1986):

> It develops as an individual acquires a conviction of personal competence, that is, when (she) believes that (she) has mastered the behaviors necessary to achieve a desired outcome. The strength of an individual's sense of self-efficacy determines whether (she) will initiate and sustain a behavior in the face of difficulties.
>
> (p. 8)

Our data demonstrated that female and male students experienced distinctly different realities in single-sex schools in comparison to when they were in coeducational schools. Although young women achieved academic success in both single-sex and coeducational settings, we observed distinct differences in young women's sense of efficacy in the two settings. Social learning had a powerful effect in the single-sex and coeducational culture. At St.

Elizabeth's young women's sense of efficacy and power was much stronger than at Xavier or at Grove when it became coeducational. We believe young women's sense of efficacy was strengthened when they were in an all-female setting that did not assert the primacy of the male.

Self-efficacy and agency are related to a sense of one's ability to control one's environment. They contribute to different positions of power for males and females in the same settings; and they seem to present different consequences for females in coeducational and all-female settings. For instance, Bryk et al. (1993) showed that women from single-sex schools had higher academic expectations and attended more selective four-year colleges than their academic qualifications would lead one to expect. At St. Elizabeth's, being female was an explicit part of the school culture; femaleness was valued. Young women were not invisible, devalued, or debased.

Our data, however, attested to the fact that young women who entered Xavier as the first wave of female students also had a strong sense of agency and efficacy. Without it, they would not have been the vanguard of coeducation. Although many asserted they were neither "feminists" nor "radicals," they were, at the very least, pioneers for the many young women who would follow them through the doors of Xavier Preparatory in the years ahead. They chose Xavier because they envisioned a proving ground for their capabilities, academically and athletically. Their vision of educational excellence was closely aligned with Xavier's male norm. As a group, they noted contradictions females experienced in the Xavier environment; for some, it was a small price to pay for a superior education; for others, it was impetus to silently retreat into quiet spaces.

One young woman from St. Elizabeth's summed up the differences between the single-sex and coed environments, demonstrating her sensitivity to effects on particular young women:

> I take care of an 8th grade girl after school, she has a lot of problems like eating disorders and depression and things like that. She is trying to decide between Xavier and St. Elizabeth's and I'm really pulling for her to go to St. Elizabeth's because I think it is a lot more stable environment. I think she would have so many problems trying to look cute all the time and trying to beat out the boys in classes and competing with boys. I think she'd be a lot happier with herself and learn a lot more about herself here. She'd be made to feel important and special here. She'd meet people that really care about her.

In our study, the value of being female was markedly greater at the all-female school than it was in the coeducational ones. Femaleness, in the coeducational center, was often devalued or simply unrecognized.

Conclusion

While Xavier and St. Elizabeth's shared similar missions for high academic standards, leadership in the community, and spirituality, the spoken rules and the unspoken assumptions about how people should behave toward authority stood in contrast to one another. Xavier emphasized uniformity and obedience to authority. It set out clear parameters of what was expected of students, enforced a dress code, and clearly explicated the "product" of good schooling. What happened at Xavier is consistent with the findings of other researchers (Bauch, 1989; Felker, 1993) who have typified a "masculine" culture emphasizing function, efficiency, and structure as compared to a more "feminine" culture that emphasizes inclusiveness, interaction, caring, and individualized learning. Young women talked about pressure to conform to the prevailing Xavier standard.

St. Elizabeth's emphasized individuality and even encouragement of some rebellion. It did not clearly articulate, as did Xavier, a "product" to be created; the rules were more flexible and, indeed, some young women from St. Elizabeth's chose to transfer to Xavier because it was "stricter." Young women at St. Elizabeth's, too, chose it for its high academic expectations and, in some cases, for sports. But over and over, they specifically mentioned their desire to be in an all-female environment where they could avoid "distractions" and "discipline problems" created by young men.

While Xavier community members became more aware of and less tolerant of sexist language and behaviors specifically, the general expectations of administrators, teachers, and students themselves did not change greatly. In sports, the Xavier goal was to offer the same opportunities for competitive sports to young women that had been available for young men, and to attract young women who would contribute to the strength of the established athletic program. The focus was on how young women might fit into existing Xavier traditions, such as the junior encounter and freshman retreat, as opposed to modifying those traditions (or starting new ones) in an attempt to best meet the needs of female students. Xavier maintained a strong focus on academic and athletic achievement and – although a sense of community had been and still is important – the atmosphere remained competitive.

Young women who chose to attend Xavier expected to have the same standards applied to them that had been applied to young men, and they expected to work hard to compete and succeed. They did not raise concerns about being dominated by young men. They accepted that they needed to have a strong voice; they accepted the expectations; they wanted to achieve at the very same level as the young men.

At Grove, the rules changed. What had been good for girls was no longer good enough. The traditions, artifacts, environment, and values that attracted young women were deemed potentially unattractive to young men. Things needed to change in order for the school to survive. The school name, spirit traditions, classroom dynamics, and power positions changed in response to the admission of the young men – in marked contrast to the experience of integrating students of the other sex at Xavier. Grove young women adapted to young men even though the young men were often academically inferior to their female counterparts.

Where cultural norms play out in unique ways beyond the direct influence of teachers and administrators, in places where girls cannot use their strongly honed academic skills to negotiate the situation, males dominate by virtue of their presence. Young women understand the appropriate places in American culture to express themselves and not express themselves. In any environment, young women must still struggle with their developing selves in a society that does not value females as much as males. But in a cloistered environment of only females, the valuing of femaleness allows them to discern its visceral qualities. They can be themselves in the fullest sense. Our experiences with the students in this study support the notion that all-female environments provide females more opportunities to become their own agents and to develop their refined sense of self-efficacy simply because the terrain of the culture is familiar – more conducive to exploring femaleness as a positive value, and simply safer for testing the feminine voice.

5   Curricular Reform, Classroom Equity

The Case of Mathematics

From the start of our study, we expressed interest in learning more about teachers' gender consciousness in the high school curriculum, particularly in mathematics. We wondered how young women's experiences in math classes differed across the three schools and whether a particular gender context might provide a "better" environment for young women to learn mathematics. We found some answers as well as new questions.

Perhaps no other high school subject has a more gendered tradition than mathematics. Despite decades of efforts to make the high school curriculum less sex-differentiated, trends continue to indicate that young women seldom enroll in secondary math courses beyond the level required for graduation (Leder, 1995). In recent years, a similar trend has surfaced as an increasing number of young women have participated in more advanced mathematics courses primarily as a means of strengthening their college applications (Dick and Rallis, 1991). Over the years, researchers have suggested a variety of reasons for different sex-based patterns of participation in mathematics such as: lack of female interest, inadequate female role models, and sex-biased high school counselors (Fennema and Carpenter, 1981; Eccles and Blumenfeld, 1985; Leder, 1992; Oakes, 1990; Stallings, 1979). Others have designed sex-equity interventions aimed at engaging young women more fully in secondary mathematics and science (Brody and Fox, 1980; Campbell and Grinstein, 1988; Harding, 1991; National Science Foundation, 1990).

In this post-Title IX era, enrollment trends indicate that an increasing percentage of high school females are taking more math than ever before (Dossey et al., 1988; Leder, 1992). A sex disparity still persists in the more advanced math courses, with males outnumbering females, sometimes by a substantial margin. Sex differences also persist in achievement (as measured on standardized tests), confidence, affinity for mathematics, and career choices related to math and science (Fennema and Carpenter, 1981; NSF, 1990; Riggs, 1988; Stanic and Hart, 1995). One notable study indicated sex differences occur even when young men and young women enroll in the same advanced math classes. Dick and Rallis (1991), using a stratified random sample of public high school seniors in Rhode Island, found that while relatively equal numbers of males and females enrolled in physics and calculus, only 18 percent of the young women versus 64 percent of the young men expressed interest in pursuing a math-related or science-related field beyond high school. Yet, on average, the young women had earned better grades than their male peers in high school. Dick and Rallis found that "being influenced by a teacher" was the only significant difference between young women who chose math and science careers and those who did not. Their finding indicates the important role that teachers and schools play in female students choosing a math-related field of study or career.

National Council of Teachers of Mathematics (NCTM) Standards

As the three schools in our study debated Xavier's coeducation decision in the late 1980s, leaders from the National Council of Teachers of Mathematics (NCTM) edited a document that would permanently alter the parameters of the sex-equity debate in K-12 mathematics. The NCTM Standards, appearing first in 1989, suggested that the math curriculum itself, traditionally abstract and disconnected from human experience, served to alienate large groups of students, particularly females. In addition, teacher delivery practices that stressed individualism and competition contributed to the idea of mathematics as an exclusive field of study, one which privileges white males more readily than any other group. The authors of the Standards called for system-wide changes in mathematics education: in the curriculum, classroom practice, teacher training, and student assessment.

Discussion of the *Curriculum and Evaluation Standards for School Mathematics* (1989) dominated the national mathematics education scene as Xavier embarked on its transition to coeducation. The NCTM Standards outlined a broad framework for what the mathematics curriculum should include in content priority and emphasis by grade level. Five general goals are central; that all students: (1) learn to value mathematics, (2) become confident in their ability to do mathematics, (3) become mathematical problem solvers, (4) learn to communicate mathematically, and (5) learn to reason mathematically. The ultimate goal is the mathematical empowerment of *all* students. The inclusive language evidences the inherent equity focus of the Standards. The call is strong and unequivocal:

> The social injustices of past schooling practices can no longer be tolerated. Current statistics indicate that those who study advanced mathematics are most often white males. Women and minorities study less mathematics and are seriously underrepresented in careers using science and technology. Creating a just society in which women and various ethnic groups enjoy equal opportunities and equitable treatment is no longer an issue. Mathematics has become a critical filter for employment and full

participation in our society. We can not afford to have the majority of our populations mathematically illiterate: Equity has become an economic necessity.

(NCTM, 1989, p.4).

This statement by the largest mathematics teachers' organization in the United States placed a new spin on mathematics reform. Mathematics education for the new millennium was about more than improving mathematical knowledge through the incorporation of technology and problem solving into the established curriculum. It required changing the curriculum to meet better the needs of traditionally excluded populations – namely women and minorities. Moreover, the message was not a suggestion but more of an ultimatum. Almost instantly, knowledge and implementation of the Standards served as a litmus test within the mathematics-reform community for addressing math equity in schools.

Confronted with the NCTM challenge, schools understandably interpreted applicability of the Standards to their situations differently. Catholic schools, in particular, tended to take a "wait and see" attitude, maintaining that the Standards applied more directly to public institutions. Others viewed the Standards as an immediate call to action. We observed similar responses among the three high schools we studied.

In this chapter, we consider how NCTM Standards were acted upon at the three schools. Through an examination of the mathematics curriculum, classroom practice, teacher beliefs, and student achievement, we explicate some of the school-specific and sex-based differences that surfaced in mathematics instruction.[1] Our discussion begins by placing our research in the context of other projects that preceded us; we continue by presenting examples of policy and practice indicative of gender awareness in mathematics education.

Previous Research on Sex Equity and Mathematics

Research on sex equity in mathematics has taken place for more than three decades. The majority of studies conducted prior to 1990 were quantitative, whereas during the 1990s there has been a strong push for more descriptive work, particularly in an effort to document classroom interactions. Today, researchers are striving to redefine the focal issues surrounding sex inequities in mathematics.

Historically, sex differences in mathematics performance, achievement, participation, and career choices have been characterized as a "girl problem." There was an unspoken assumption that girls were somehow deficient, incapable of performing in mathematics at the same level as their male counterparts (Campbell, 1995). Most recently, results indicate that much of the sex-based variation in achievement and mathematics enrollment has diminished at the secondary level. However, important and statistically significant sex differences still persist. Sex differences remain notable and disturbing in females' low participation in advanced mathematics courses and subsequent restricted career choices. In response, educators and researchers alike have designed interventions that provide girls some of what they are seemingly missing, such as: experience with manipulatives and other mathematical tools, extra encouragement about their own mathematical ability, exposure to female role models, and additional opportunities to discuss mathematics.

Others believe, however, these strategies may be merely temporary solutions. Critics maintain that helping young women build skills and experiences for better negotiating the secondary mathematics curriculum may produce positive short-term results; but once the young women return to a less-friendly environment for any extended time, the positive effects fade and eventually disappear. Instead, many advocates for sex equity in mathematics recommend a change in tactic: to fundamentally change the mathematics that is being taught, rather than continuing to focus on the deficiency theory of girls (Campbell, 1995; Secada et al., 1995; Noddings, 1998). They advocate for curricular reform that gives female students opportunities to construct their own mathematical meanings. The reformers' vision for mathematics instruction emphasizes the use of cooperative learning instead of individual competition and focuses on mathematical connections to the world. The National Council of Teachers of Mathematics (NCTM) Standards for the curriculum, evaluation, and teaching have certainly played a role in shaping such efforts. Coincidentally, the publications of the NCTM Standards fortuitously coincided with the transitions occurring in the three schools we studied.

The Mathematics Curriculum

At the outset of our research, all three high schools offered a traditional, calculus-driven curriculum that began with pre-algebra and culminated with Advanced Placement (AP) calculus, for those students who continued in mathematics. No school offered upper-division alternatives, such as probability and statistics. The vast majority of 9th graders at all three schools completed at least a three-year sequence of mathematics that began with algebra, followed by geometry in the 10th grade, and algebra II in the 11th grade. Many students also went on to study pre-calculus in the 12th grade. More advanced students generally began with geometry and finished with calculus at the end of four years. Remedial students enrolled in pre-algebra as 9th graders, and if they continued in mathematics, could graduate at the algebra II level, a requirement for admission to the state university. During 1993–1994, all three schools provided eligible students the opportunity to take the AP calculus test, although students were more strongly encouraged to take the exam by teachers in some schools than in others.

As we began our study, the St. Elizabeth's faculty chose to break with tradition and undertake a major curricular change in mathematics. Their motivations were two-fold: (1) to respond to the administration's expressed wish for all departments to incorporate concepts from *Women's Ways of Knowing* (Belenky et al., 1986) into their instruction, and (2) to begin addressing the nationally based directive contained in the NCTM Standards. In spring, 1991, after much deliberation among themselves and with the administration, the St. Elizabeth's math department chose to abandon its more traditional pedagogy, opting to implement a reform-minded secondary mathematics curriculum in September 1991. The new curriculum called for adopting a new series of textbooks, commonly referred to as "the Chicago Series," hailed at that time as extremely innovative progressive texts, particularly with respect to incorporating the NCTM Standards.[2]

The Chicago Series encourages an integrated strategy for teaching secondary mathematics with equal emphasis on reading, writing, and problem solving. With the use of technology and applications woven throughout, the Chicago Series focuses on four areas of mathematical understanding: (1) learning skills in carrying out various algorithms; (2) developing and using mathematical properties and relationships; (3) applying mathematics in realistic situations; and (4) representing or picturing mathematical concepts.[3] St. Elizabeth's made the commitment to implement the Chicago Series and planned to introduce the new curriculum slowly. In fall, 1991, only the 9th graders used the new books. Every succeeding year, another grade was added until the fall of 1994, when AP calculus was replaced with a course called discrete mathematics and the faculty decided to offer calculus no longer.[4] Discontinuing calculus was an understandably difficult decision for a college preparatory institution such as St. Elizabeth's. Administrators, parents, and students alike expressed skepticism. Based on recommendations of the National Council of Teachers of Mathematics (NCTM) and the Mathematics Association of America (MAA), the faculty believed it was the right decision for St. Elizabeth's and defended its new direction:

> We understand that such a low percentage of students actually go on to calculus that we are doing them a disservice by only preparing them for calculus. The discrete mathematics, FST this year and discrete mathematics and pre-calculus next year, takes them thoroughly through the pre-college mathematics that they need. Forget the calculus. Eighty-five percent will never go on to calculus. But almost all of them will have to take more math! Either statistics or some other area.
>
> female teacher, St. Elizabeth's

They were successful. Beginning with the 1994–1995 school year, St. Elizabeth's became the only Catholic high school in the region that did not offer calculus – perhaps a dubious honor – especially for an all-female school. To understand the curricular decisions of St. Elizabeth's mathematics department requires deeper knowledge of the national reform efforts in math education during the early 1990s. Recall that the NCTM Standards were hardly a year old when St. Elizabeth's embarked on its reform path. They were not only making a major change, but putting themselves on the cutting edge of secondary mathematics education.

The Calculus Decision: The Role of the NCTM Standards

One highly controversial curricular component of the Standards is the decreased emphasis on some topics that were once considered essentials of the secondary mathematics curriculum. Examples of the core topics receiving decreased emphasis include: conic sections, pencil and paper graphing by point plotting or tables, Euclidean geometry as a complete axiomatic system, and trigonometric identities. In addition, the Standards do *not* advocate formal teaching of calculus at the secondary level, even for college-bound students:

> Rather the Standards call for opportunities for students to systematically, but informally, investigate the central ideas of calculus–limit, the area under a curve, the rate of change, and the slope of a tangent line – that contribute to a deepening of their understanding of function and its utility in representing and answering questions about real world problems. ... Instructional activities should be aimed at providing students with firm conceptual underpinnings of calculus rather than at developing manipulative techniques.
>
> (NCTM, 1989, p180)

Thus, the Standards suggest that high school math teachers focus on teaching their students the conceptual foundations of calculus rather than calculus itself. That recommendation is based on an assumption that "scientific calculators with graphing capabilities will be available to all students at all times" (NCTM, 1989, p. 124). Only with access to computers or scientific calculators with graphing capabilities could the foundations of calculus be taught in such an exploratory fashion.

Calculators and Computers

In the last decade, the availability of new technology has changed the nature of mathematical problems addressed in schools. The authors of the NCTM Standards recognized the value of that technology and advocated the availability of appropriate calculators for all students, as well as access to computers for mathematics work. Our questionnaire data indicated that students at all three high schools were using calculators regularly for their mathematics studies. During our classroom observations, we noted nearly all St. Elizabeth's students not only had a calculator, but a specific kind, the Texas Instruments (TI) graphics calculator. Their bright blue plastic cases were easy to spot. We began looking for TI graphics calculators during observations at other sites. Although we saw some, we seldom saw a classroom where all students had one, as appeared to be the case at St. Elizabeth's. We interviewed St. Elizabeth's teachers and asked about the calculators. Indeed, all upper-division students were required to have a TI-81 graphing calculator. The math department had devised a "rent-to-own" program for those who found the cost of the calculator (approximately $85) prohibitive. Students could pay for the calculator over time, $20 per semester.

Grove students were not generally encouraged to use calculators and those we saw were more scientific calculators; we saw only six Grove students with graphics calculators in all of our observations. At Xavier, third and fourth year math students were encouraged, but not required to use graphics calculators. The math department at Xavier had purchased an overhead version of the TI-81. We observed it in use twice. We were surprised that Xavier would invest in such an expensive piece of equipment prior to students having individual access to the hand-held version. In some respect, however, the decision to invest in the overhead equipment was in keeping with a Xavier educational philosophy of "learning by watching" as opposed to "learning by doing." Contrary to what occurred on Xavier's athletic playing fields, the learning of mathematics appeared to be more of a spectator sport.

Course Offerings

Table 5.1 provides a listing of mathematics offerings in each school. Given the differences in the schools' student body sizes by 1993–1994, we expected to see differences in the number of mathematics sections offered across sites. However, Table 5.1 indicates some important variations in the basic number of courses being offered as well as how those courses were distributed across the curriculum. For example, both St. Elizabeth's and Grove offered a greater variety of courses at the lower end of the curriculum. Xavier, on the other hand, offered more upper-division mathematics, notably second-year calculus, a course which explicitly prepared students for the second level of the Advanced Placement calculus exam. Grove and St. Elizabeth's (prior to the curriculum change) offered calculus courses that prepared students for the first level only. Notice St. Elizabeth's offered the greatest number of different math courses (twelve distinct classes in total), while Grove offered the least, with nine different math classes.

A closer examination of Table 5.1 indicates that a greater number of math offerings at St. Elizabeth's meant more tracking as well as an attempt to accommodate students with lower levels of mathematics achievement. For example, there were three different geometry classes at St. Elizabeth's during 1993–1994, basic geometry, geometry, and honors geometry. Xavier and Grove offered only two, geometry, and honors geometry. St. Elizabeth's third course, "basic geometry," was a watered-down version of geometry designed to serve the needs of students whom teachers suspected would struggle in the standard course. Enrolling in "basic geometry" as a sophomore, however, made it impossible for a student to take pre-calculus before graduation and unlikely that she would enroll in algebra II – thereby limiting future educational and career options requiring math. Neither Grove nor Xavier offered "basic geometry" but remediated students by placing them in a course one year behind their grade-level peers. In an effort to meet the learning needs of their female students, St. Elizabeth's had inadvertently created paths of lower-level math achievement for young women. While the St. Elizabeth's faculty and administration argued that "basic geometry" exists to keep young women interested in math, there were unintended and unforeseen consequences.

Table 5.1 Mathematics Course Offerings by School

Course Title	No. of Sections at Xavier	No. of Sections at St. Elizabeth's	No. of Sections at Grove
Pre-Algebra / Intro. to Algebra	2	1	1
Basic Algebra I	–	–	–
Algebra I	6	3	4
Honors Algebra I (Alg. I Accelerated)	3	1	–
Basic Geometry	–	1	–
Geometry	6	4	2
Honors Geometry (Geom. Accelerated)	3	1	1
Algebra II Topics (remedial)	–	1	–
Algebra II (Advanced Algebra)	5	3	2
Honors Algebra II	–	1	1
Pre-Calculus (FST[a], Elem. Funct.)	2	2	1
Honors Pre-Calculus	1	1	1
Pre-Calculus Accelerated	4	–	–
Calculus (first-year)[b]	3	1	1
Calculus (second-year)	1	–	–
Total	36	22	14

Notes:
a FST = Functions, Statistics, and Trigonometry w/ Computers, a course based on the Chicago Series, offered only at St. Elizabeth's.
b St. Elizabeth's no longer offered Calculus following the 1993–1994 school year.

The Role of Tracking

All three schools employed a three-track system for math. Xavier offered the fewest low-end options in mathematics. For example, a 9th grader might enroll in pre-algebra, but that student would go on to algebra I in the 10th grade and geometry in the 11th grade. Xavier offered no remedial option, such as the watered-down "basic geometry" course at St. Elizabeth's. The mathematics curriculum at Xavier had the most differentiated advanced courses in mathematics. Xavier placed a premium on accelerating students in hopes of getting as many to calculus as possible before graduation. To this end, there were two types of pre-calculus courses offered: a grade-level pre-calculus course, entitled "elementary functions," and an accelerated course called "accelerated pre-calculus" that followed the geometry year. This later calculus class combined the material from a traditional second-year algebra course and a high school pre-calculus class into a single year, enabling many students to reach the second-year calculus level as seniors. All students in the class were either sophomores or juniors, and while the strategy may succeed in getting students to calculus, it could be pushing students too hard, too fast.

Tracking in mathematics affects more than math. Although all schools reported grouping students heterogeneously in subject areas such as English, religion, and social studies, examination of the student survey data (collected during these courses) indicated clusters of students in the same math and science track and with similar Grade Point Averages (GPAs), suggesting that students placed in particular math or science tracks also took other classes together despite those being officially "untracked courses." As a result, during a school day, students generally interacted with a small subset of peers in their grade level. A number of students in our focus groups across the three schools complained about this phenomenon. One young woman's comments reflect the student frustrations best:

> Like right now I'm in all honors classes and that means that I end up taking all of my classes with all the same people all day. Because our class only has like 82 people and a lot of them I never see because I don't have any classes with them. ... It gets more selective as you go. ... And it makes me sad that there are people that you just kind of lose touch with.
>
> Student, St. Elizabeth's

Because of the small size of these three schools, tracking in math necessitated tracking in other subjects. With a limited number of students, teachers, and classes, the schedule simply did not allow for both tracked and mixed groupings. Understandably, this issue became less of a problem at Xavier after coeducation increased the school's size, but Xavier also had more limited mathematics offerings initially.

Table 5.2 shows the actual distribution of students in mathematics tracks across schools. Math placements necessarily result in differential mathematics learning opportunities for students at the three schools. Two things are immediately apparent by pursuing data in the table. First, in comparison to Xavier and Grove, students at St. Elizabeth's were more equally distributed across the three tracks. Second, St. Elizabeth's had the highest percentage of students in its remedial track and the lowest in honors. The other two schools had smaller remedial tracks, with more students in the regular and honors tracks. We think the fact that St. Elizabeth's offered more remedial options led to more students in the remedial track; the general rule being if a school creates a track, students will fill it. Grove and Xavier, on the other hand, placed students in the remedial track less frequently and by putting them in courses a year behind grade level. At Grove, the track with the highest percentage enrollment was the honors track. At Xavier, the regular and honors track were essentially identical in size, with only 10 percent of the 11th and 12th graders in a remedial math program.

Catholic schools commonly use ability grouping. One primary difference between tracks in Catholic schools versus those in public schools, however, is that in Catholic schools, students are more likely assigned to their track by teachers or counselors whereas often in public schools students make the choice (Bryk et al., 1993). The faculty members in Catholic schools take greater responsibility for student distribution across tracks. The math department faculties of the three high schools confirmed this fact, explaining that students' 9th grade math placements were made based on grades, entrance exam scores, 8th grade teacher recommendations, and, in borderline cases, the view of the students and his or her parents.

While a possibility exists that students can switch tracks during their high school career, such changes are highly unlikely. Once schools place a student in a particular track, that is where he or she remains throughout high school (Oakes, 1985). Among the students in our study, less than 5 percent of the students changed tracks; an equal number moved down as moved up.

Table 5.2 Mathematics Track Placement by School Site

Math Track	Percentage of Students Enrolled at Xavier	Percentage of Students Enrolled at St. Elizabeth's	Percentage of Students Enrolled at Grove
Remedial	10.2	29.5	16.7
Regular	44.7	35.6	40.2
Honors	44.4	34.9	41.2

How do the different tracks afford students different learning opportunities? Some researchers argue students in Catholic school tracks do not have substantially different academic experiences whereas public school tracks provide very different academic experiences (NCEA, 1985; Bryk et al., 1993). They claim the tracking system in Catholic schools does not have the extreme variations in academic opportunities one sees in public schools. However, we take issue with that point based on the experience with our three schools. For example, the algebra II classes across all sites suffered from problems associated with required courses. They tended to attract students with lower motivation and weaker math skills. As a result, algebra II classes were far less rigorous; they exhibited the most traditional pedagogical structures and had the most discipline problems. Thus, our three schools suffered problems endemic to tracking; less was demanded of the students in the lower-level classes, and the gap increased between those in the remedial track and those in the advanced track over their school years.

Beliefs and Practices of Mathematics Teachers

We interviewed all mathematics teachers teaching upper-division courses from the three schools at least twice and observed each of them teaching at least three times. Ten teachers participated, four women and six men; five Xavier teachers, three St. Elizabeth's teachers, and two teachers from Grove. Teachers often espoused their views about mathematics teaching and mathematics as a discipline, and many talked about the current reform movement, the NCTM Standards, and about the Chicago Series that was being used at St. Elizabeth's. They held a variety of views about mathematics. Whereas some voiced the traditional point of view seeing math as a collection of cumulative, but disparate topics or ideas with a strong emphasis on objectivity; others assumed a more modern view, seeing mathematics as a coherent language for problem solving and as a tool for analyzing open-ended questions. A teacher's mathematical philosophy was generally positively correlated to his or her views on the reform movement in mathematics education; those traditional teachers were opposed while the more progressive teachers were in favor.

Teachers' Philosophical View of Mathematics

All Xavier math teachers expressed a more traditional view of mathematics and mathematics teaching; they were generally committed to the calculus-driven tradition that had served the school successfully for decades. Changing that tradition, as some teachers indicated, would be difficult.

> I think anytime you change in a curriculum like math where there are clear building blocks, it's tough.
>
> female teacher, Xavier

We teach to the Advanced Placement curriculum really, which is a traditional calculus curriculum and I'd like to see Xavier move more toward an integrated math curriculum. But I haven't seen any integrated curriculum that allows one to do two years of calculus in high school. In fact, most of them so de-emphasize calculus that if you don't get to it in high school, that's fine. And that wouldn't bother me at all. But I think a school like Xavier has such advanced kids that you could still teach calculus, but probably not two years of it.

male teacher, Xavier

St. Elizabeth's teachers, on the other hand, expressed a progressive view of mathematics reflecting their commitment to the NCTM Standards and the use of the Chicago Series. One of the teachers summarized the view of her colleagues:

I see us actually moving toward kind of a new era in mathematics teaching. I see mathematics as being the center of how you learn to problem solve and how that then carries over into all the subject areas, no matter what the subject areas, but I can see us as being experts in how you problem solve.

female teacher, St. Elizabeth's

Grove teachers expressed more variation, and no consensus, in their philosophy of math and their views on reforms. One teacher shared a particular view about the confused status of mathematics.

They hear their parents say, "Oh, don't worry, I wasn't very good in math either." I mean, it's like the joke, the American joke, "Well, I wasn't very good in math." You never hear anybody say, "Well, I was never any good at reading," because they're just too embarrassed about it. And then there's the whole technical thing, I mean I guess math is seen as something that's going to lead you in this direction. And I guess reading is seen as more general. But I really think math has so many more uses than people realize.

male teacher, Grove

Taken together, math teachers' views in our study indicated the present views about mathematics education generally. Historically, mathematics has been a highly selective field based on mastering techniques and the utilization of purely objective measures. The current shift toward a more integrated discipline emphasizes multiple methods that students apply to real-life problems. Reform advocates stress that success in an increasingly technically based society demands this reconceptualization of mathematics.

Teachers' View of the NCTM Standards and Reform Efforts in Mathematics Education

Some teachers talked more about the NCTM Standards than their own view of mathematics. In 1993–1994 the Standards were almost four years old. While some teachers were just learning of their content, others were trying to implement the Standards (NCTM, 1994).

> We're so embroiled in the Standards and the different kind of changes that we are having to make in what we teach the students and how we try to get them to think and I don't think that the other teachers in the other disciplines realize what's going on.
>
> female teacher, St. Elizabeth's

During 1993–1994 St. Elizabeth's teachers were in the midst of implementation and articulated some of the struggles they were having in carrying out such a major transition. They were in sharp contrast to their counterparts at Xavier, who rhetorically professed to be adopting the Standards but had not yet taken action.

> Well, we were the first school to take the NCTM Standards to the archdiocese. When all the publications first came out, there was a meeting at the pastoral center for math chairmen, one representative from each math department, and we took along the NCTM Standards. And most people had not seen them at that point. So what we've tried to do is with the textbooks that we have, we've tried to emphasize the things that are part of the NCTM Standards. I really think that's why we decided to go with the ... book because it does address some of the Standards in a way that the other books did not.
>
> female teacher, Xavier

That Xavier was the first to bring the Standards to the diocese was ironic. Of the three sites, Xavier was the least likely to stray from its highly traditional curriculum. Indeed, during our numerous classroom observations at Xavier, there was little evidence of the Standards in place excepting the sporadic presence of graphics calculators and group work in a few classes. Even the textbooks selected by the Xavier math department incorporated the Standards only at the most minimal level. The youngest math teacher at Xavier spoke about the textbook selection and the school's traditional approach to math.

> I student taught with the Chicago Series. I kind of liked it, but I mean that's a little more innovative than, I mean it's just kind of a newer trend in math I suppose. And this [points to current text] is ... well ... although, it's you know, what am I trying to say. It's not as advanced.

It's not trying to hit the Standards like the Chicago Series. So I don't think the kids have a problem with it because it's more of the traditional thing that they are used to.

male teacher, Xavier

This young teacher's comments underscore two critical points with respect to this study: (1) Xavier's strong commitment to its traditional curriculum, and (2) the extent to which the Chicago Series had become a recognized vehicle for implementing the NCTM Standards.

The University Of Chicago Series

A team of educators including college professors and high school and elementary teachers developed the Chicago Series in conjunction with the NCTM Standards. The first edition appeared in 1990, directly on the heels of the publication of NCTM's first Standards volume. The high school texts, especially, were markedly different from anything that teachers and students had used previously. Colorful pages incorporating numerous applications, an integrated approach, the utilization of computers and other technology, and an emphasis on reading and writing made these books a model for implementing secondary mathematics reform.

The mathematics department at St. Elizabeth's formally adopted the books in the fall of 1990 after months of study and debate. Almost four years into their implementation, they still expressed enthusiasm for the series.

I love it! I think what I really like about it is that every year I teach out of it, I like it more, which is different from every other book that I've ever taught out of. What I like about the materials is that they do what they say they are trying to do, where they change the focus just slightly so that they're not asking rote questions. They are really asking questions that come from just a slightly different angle. And they don't just give them the answer. They have them think about and lead them on sometimes and try to get them to come to some sort of understanding instead of just the crank out – here's a problem, work it out ...

female teacher, St. Elizabeth's

The other thing that I want to say in favor of our particular math department ... when we first started is that we were encouraged to use the tool, not just use the book. We were encouraged to read what the philosophy of the book was and to try to use it as it was intended to be used. Whereas, I talk to teachers in other schools and one said, "Well, I'll use this chapter and I'll use that chapter," and they've gone ahead and used it in their own teaching style, so you always adapt to your teaching style but the tool always has other things there for you to try to use too. For example, doing all of the review problems instead of just skipping them. I think that has been really a big part of our success.

female teacher, St. Elizabeth's

The St. Elizabeth's math faculty recognized from the outset that use of the Chicago Series would require a significant adjustment by teachers and students. Teachers would need to facilitate more than demonstrate; students would need to learn independently and to use their peers as resources rather than relying so heavily on teachers as the sources of knowledge.

> I don't know if I like the role, but I like what happens to the kids. I'd like to just get up there and do the whole thing. I enjoy that kind of thing. So I have had to learn to appreciate this new role that I have. ... [referring to students] We have quite a few of those who get through school by being the best spellers and memorizing the grammar and memorizing formulas and seeing patterns and they just want to go on and do that and they don't like this book.

female teacher, St. Elizabeth's

St. Elizabeth's math teachers reported adapting to the Chicago Series had not been without struggle or challenge. Having persevered, they believed their efforts were worthwhile. They exhibited pride in what they accomplished in implementing such a Standards-driven curriculum.

Even teachers who had never used the Chicago Series had an opinion given the high profile, at times controversial, reputation of the texts. They generally expressed more skeptical views.

> I'm a little concerned about that University of Chicago series and whether the kids get enough repetition. ... They seem to have a generalized knowledge of a lot of things, but not the depth that you get with maybe a more traditional curriculum.

female teacher, Xavier

Grove math teachers' voices were noticeably absent in explicit references to NCTM Standards, mathematics reform, and the Chicago Series. While they were aware of the Standards, they did not take a stand as a faculty but instead functioned as independent agents in their classrooms. At Grove we observed one teacher whose methods reflected the Standards and another who was not reform minded.

> I mean there are probably other ways to teach it ... you know, but there's a lot of people talking about the new methods and stuff like that. And I've tried some of the things and I think it's good to bring it up but

I think it always comes back to kids just need to learn the basic skills and the way you do that is by practicing.

> male teacher, Grove

A theme that emerges from this inquiry is that major curricular reform agendas remain difficult, even under the best circumstances. A national reform movement such as the NCTM Standards yields disparate results. Some schools and teachers ignored the effort as distant, disconnected, and inapplicable to them or their students, as seemed to be the case at Grove. Others took issue with the call for change, proclaiming success with the old method; as at Xavier. Others embraced the change, as did the St. Elizabeth's math faculty, believing the Standards responded to some of their sex-equity concerns.

Women Teaching Math

The female and male math teachers we studied differed notably in their interview responses and teaching philosophies. They were also distributed unevenly across the three schools in 1993–1994. Overwhelmingly, men taught upper-division mathematics at Grove and Xavier. At Grove, all mathematics courses were taught by men. At Xavier, male math teachers outnumbered female math teachers by a ratio of 2:1 and men taught most of the advanced classes. Department chairs at Xavier and Grove, the transitional schools, were men. St. Elizabeth's had no male math teachers.

Each female math teacher at Xavier and St. Elizabeth's alluded to her position as a woman in a field dominated by men. Some recounted the differential treatment encountered as a high school student.

> When I was in high school, I did not enjoy math, and as a woman, I was not encouraged to take math.
>
> female teacher, Xavier

> In high school, I didn't really get any pats on the back. I mean I got A's but ... [pause] ... our teacher did take six people out of our class and take them over to the university to take calculus our senior year, but only one of those was a female and her father was a professor of mathematics at the university. But I didn't ever say anything, I just figured I wasn't good enough to go. And then, we had our twenty-fifth reunion and I ran into her and two other women who ended up majoring in math who were not picked to go and we said, "You know we really ran circles around those guys in math." But at the time, I didn't question it. My parents didn't question it.
>
> female teacher, St. Elizabeth's

Yet, these female math teachers gave credit to their teachers, both male and female, who had encouraged their mathematical pursuits. Female teachers reflected particularly fondly about female teachers who had supported them. All of these women had more male math teachers than female math teachers when they were high school students. They said the mathematics path they had chosen had not been easy. They recognized the young women in their classes would need to work hard and persevere if they were to succeed in mathematical fields.

> And maybe I kind of push too much but I know when I went to college that was one of things that all of a sudden it all kind of clicked and I had just gone through the motions in high school. And I'll tell you, I'll be honest with you, and being a female I can say this, that it really bothers me when a girl who's getting a B, 85 percent, a pretty solid B, chooses the easy way out, it bothers me. And you can do whatever you want to do and she can do whatever she wants to do, but that really bothers me. I think that is what all the studies say, we tried to get the girls to go for it and if there's any kind of uneasiness, then they don't want to face that and that bothers me.
>
> female teacher, Xavier

For all of them, however, pursuing mathematics meant being a survivor. It required considerable commitment and risk-taking. Not one teacher expressed regrets about becoming a math teacher, but rather they exhibited pride about being math teachers, and most especially a *female* math teacher.

St. Elizabeth's all-female mathematics department readily expressed self-satisfaction in being women in mathematics, and also being members of an all-female math department. They believed the sex composition of their group afforded them possibilities that would not be available had the faculty included men. Indeed, St. Elizabeth's math department exhibited cohesiveness unmatched in the other schools.[5] They spoke of sharing assignments, exchanging teaching strategies, teaching each other new material, and making collective decisions. Together, they formed a team with purpose.

> This is probably going to come off sounding about as sexist as you can be, but I think that because we're an all-women math department, I think that women sometimes are willing to go out on a limb and try the new book. I think that some of our ... well ... colleagues in ... well ... they have told us things like, "I've been teaching math for thirty years and I'll be damned if I'm going to learn something new." I always remember something someone said up in Leland [site of the most recent NCTM regional meeting]: if women had been the mathematicians, would mathematics look different than it does today? I think it would. I think

we're much more practical. And I don't think that there would be this constant association with war and mechanics.

female teacher, St. Elizabeth's

While not all women math teachers spoke so passionately about their roles as educators, the female math teachers at Xavier and St. Elizabeth's shared a common understanding of their unique position as women in mathematics. They wanted mathematics to be an inclusive endeavor, contrary to the exclusivity they had experienced as teenagers. It was primarily in the classrooms of female teachers that we saw cooperative learning, inclusive classroom practice, organized group-work activities, and students participating in the design of assignments.

Classroom Practice

Instructional practice in mathematics classrooms varied as much from teacher to teacher as across schools. Only at St. Elizabeth's did teachers exhibit consensus about mathematics pedagogy. Even at St. Elizabeth's, however, teachers varied in their styles of presentation, use of technology, and amount of independent study time. Distinct patterns emerged across the three schools; there were differences in teachers' questioning of students, lesson organization, student group work, opportunities for student presentations, collection of homework, and use of technology.

Xavier students had the fewest opportunities to put mathematical ideas into their own words, the least amount of group work, fewest student presentations, and the most teacher-centered lecture and discussion sessions. Both Xavier and Grove teachers used class time for presenting new material. St. Elizabeth's was almost the opposite of Xavier and Grove; math teachers encouraged students in math dialogue, used small-group work, and spent the least amount of class time on learning new material. It was common for students at St. Elizabeth's and Grove to present solutions to problems at the overhead or chalkboard; something we never observed at Xavier. At Xavier, students were almost always seated in rows, listening to the teacher for the entire period. Nightly homework assignments were collected at Xavier many times each week, at Grove once or twice a week, and at St. Elizabeth's about twice per month. St. Elizabeth's math teachers, however, assigned long-term problem-based assignments in projects and reports.

Teaching differences attributed to sex, in our limited study, must be tempered with a knowledge of the distribution of males and females across the three math faculties. Overall, male teachers expressed more traditional views of mathematics than their female counterparts, and this view carried over into classroom practice. Women in the study tended to be interested in alternative pedagogy, particularly in permitting students to work in groups or assigning long-term mathematical projects. There were exceptions to these generalizations. Two of the male teachers in the study exhibited instances of formal group work in their teaching: one at Xavier and one at Grove.[6] Other male teachers permitted students to work collectively, but did not organize cooperative group activities.

How did teachers' classroom practices reflect the vision of the NCTM Standards? In the second volume of its *Standards, professional standards for teaching mathematics* (1991), NCTM offered a vision of teaching that supports the curricular changes outlined in their 1989 publication. They described five major shifts in classroom practice necessary for moving mathematics teaching toward NCTM's vision for the country's mathematical future. These five shifts are represented in Table 5.3.

From our data, we concluded that only St. Elizabeth's teachers were working toward a Standards-based vision of math education at the time of the study. Unlike most of their colleagues elsewhere, St. Elizabeth's math teachers relinquished some of their authority in order to learn along with their students. Topics such as computer-assisted graphing and statistics necessitated such a participatory change. Still, even within St. Elizabeth's, there was variation across classes.

Table 5.4 summarizes the extent to which we observed schools offering activities recommended by the NCTM Standards. St. Elizabeth's made a strong showing, although all schools studied show modest evidence of meeting some NCTM Standards. Table 5.4 suggests the greatest disparities across sites were in using technology and the integration of math subjects within courses, with St. Elizabeth's far ahead of the other schools.

St. Elizabeth's math faculty created classroom learning environments that included student opportunities for mathematical dialogue, experiences with technology, exposure to extensive real-world applications, and an emphasis on reading and writing about mathematics. However, the pedagogically progressive and well-intentioned experiences at St. Elizabeth's Academy did not lead to high achievement outcomes for those students, in comparison to their female peers who attended the other two schools. Instead, St.

Table 5.3 Classroom Changes Encouraged by the NCTM Standards

Classroom Element	Pre-Standards	Post-Standards
Class functions as ...	a collection of individuals	a mathematical community
Teacher serves as ...	the authority for answers	the facilitator of student activity
Learning is based on ...	memorizing procedures	mathematical reasoning
Activity involves ...	rote, mechanistic answer finding	conjecturing, problem-solving
Math conceived as ...	a body of isolated ideas	connections, applications

Table 5.4 *Classroom Activities Suggested by the NCTM Standards and Evidence of their Presence at the Three Sites*

Activity Suggested by the Standards	Site-Based Evidence		
	Xavier	St. Elizabeth's	Grove
hands-on manipulative activities	–	√	√
applications to daily life	√	√	√
concrete experiences before abstract treatments	☆	☆	☆
students working in groups	√	+	√
student presenting mathematics to peers	–	+	√
taking student preconceptions into account when planning	√	√	√
use of computers	–	+	–
use of calculators*	+	+	√
integration of mathematics subjects	–	+	–
deeper coverage of fewer concepts	☆	☆	☆

Notes:
– no evidence
☆ insufficient evidence
√ modest evidence
+ strong evidence
* especially graphics calculators at secondary level

Elizabeth's students had lower SAT scores and math grades, achieved a lower level of mathematics attainment, expressed less interest in mathematics, and were more likely to discontinue their math studies prior to graduation than their female counterparts at Xavier and Grove. The following section provides more details about these findings with some analysis to explain the disparity between uplifting and engaging classroom experiences and conventional performance-based outcome measures.

Student Achievement

St. Elizabeth's Academy seemed to be doing everything right to encourage the mathematical development of its female students. The young women had strong female role models; they were taught solely by women who enjoyed mathematics and who had committed their lives' work to teaching it at the secondary level. The school adopted a curriculum in alignment with the NCTM Standards. Students had experience with problem solving and real-life applications. They talked about mathematics in small-group discussions and in presentations to their peers. They engaged in alternative assessments and learned to work with technology as a mathematical tool. All had some experience writing computer programs to solve mathematical problems.

Given those positive conditions at St. Elizabeth's, one would anticipate strong achievement outcomes. Yet, according to the data from students' academic transcripts, St. Elizabeth's young women, compared to their counterparts at Xavier and Grove, had lower SAT math scores and math GPAs and were more likely to drop mathematics prior to graduation.

Table 5.5 summarizes a handful of the math achievement outcomes examined in this study. Note that in the first year of coeducation, Xavier young women indicated the highest level of math attainment; they came to Xavier with strong math backgrounds and were placed into high-level advanced courses. Overall, Grove young women had the strongest math achievement outcomes, the highest math SAT scores, combined with a high level of math attainment and a strong persistence rate – 79 percent of the females in the graduating classes of 1994 and 1995 at Grove enrolled in a fourth year of mathematics.

As we shared our findings with the schools, the comparatively poor performance of the young women from St. Elizabeth's proved both surprising and unnerving. The math SAT scores were somewhat expected because the national norm-referenced exam did not align well with the new reform-minded curriculum. The faculty at St. Elizabeth's also has a reputation for being tough graders, hence, the lower math GPAs. Yet, the administration and faculty at St. Elizabeth's were particularly dismayed with so many students dropping math before graduation. Their perception was that essentially "all" students at St. Elizabeth's completed four full years of mathematics. In fact, nearly 40 percent of the young women dropped math during high school. Since they adopted the Chicago Series in an effort to make mathematics more attractive to female students, the administration and faculty were deeply frustrated the data indicated otherwise.

The principal speculated about two reasons for this phenomenon. First,

Table 5.5 Comparative Achievement Outcomes for Females Only Across Sites

Outcome	Xavier	St. Elizabeth's	Grove
Mean math level attained*	4.15	3.55	3.94
Mean SAT math score	528.09	496.86	539.33
Mean SAT verbal score	494.68	505.33	488.67
Percentage enrolling in 4 years of math	66.0	59.3	79.7

*Value represents the equivalent of the number of years of study beyond pre-algebra

St. Elizabeth's, with its location in the heart of the down town area, attracted students from more diverse socioeconomic and ethnic backgrounds than Xavier or Grove, which might contribute to students' failure to persist in mathematics. Second, the minimal number of electives (only 1.5 semester credits in four years) at St. Elizabeth's forced students to make tough choices. The principal viewed the math teachers as "caring and committed," but not as popular with students as those in other departments, such as science, where teachers used experiential methods and offered students hands-on research opportunities. However, when we tested the principal's hypotheses statistically there was little support for the demographic theory by social class or race, nor for the selectivity hypothesis. According to the transcript data, students were not taking science during the senior year as a replacement for math.

A third hypothesis we researchers offered was the role of tracking at St. Elizabeth's. Our conjecture proved fruitful. An examination of the three tracks indicated that 59 percent of the young women who enrolled in the regular track at St. Elizabeth's dropped math prior to graduation. Moreover, the regular track was the largest of the three. The drop rates for the other two tracks were significantly lower: 37.9 percent for the remedial track and 26.7 percent for the honors track ($X^2 = 9.16$, df $= 2$, p $< .05$). It appeared that in an atmosphere of limited academic choices, St. Elizabeth's students, particularly those in the regular track, did not view mathematics as an attractive option. The majority of young women in the regular track chose not to study mathematics as seniors.

Perhaps their decision was legitimate, especially for students with a desire to pursue other interests such as science, creative writing, sports, or theater. The comparatively high numbers of senior St. Elizabeth's students who did not continue their math education remained bothersome. St. Elizabeth's principal expressed curiosity and gratitude when we shared this finding. She believed that perhaps those counseling young women were not encouraging students to opt for the fourth year in math as much as before. Yet according to our questionnaire data, St. Elizabeth's students reported being encouraged to take math more than any other group. Still, there must have been some truth to the principal's speculation because within two years of this study the math drop rate was reduced from 40 percent to 27 percent and it has remained in the 25–30 percent range.

Applying the Gender Consciousness Continuum to the Case of Mathematics

More than other teachers in the study, St. Elizabeth's math faculty expressed keen awareness of females' historical exclusion from full participation in the secondary math curriculum and the restrictive implications for young women's career choices. They viewed implementation of the NCTM

Standards as a nationally sanctioned means of developing a new curriculum that would meaningfully engage young women in the study of mathematics. As they immersed themselves in the implementation, the math faculty's enthusiasm for the new textbooks and curriculum took on an almost religious zeal. They attempted new teaching strategies and learned new topics, such as statistics and probability, in which none of them had training. We found this particularly admirable. The women of St. Elizabeth's Academy were pioneers, like their founders. With the Chicago Series as their guide and graphics calculators as their weapon, they ventured into new mathematical territory.

There are always risks associated with implementing innovation in schools, particularly when that innovation is a new curriculum. St. Elizabeth's was not immune to those risks. On the contrary, it was especially vulnerable. As an all-female institution attempting to counter the deeply embedded sex-based stereotypes in a field traditionally dominated by men, the school had an even narrower margin of error.

We will never know the precise reasons for the math achievement and attitudinal differences that surfaced among the young women attending Xavier, St. Elizabeth's, and Grove during the 1993–1994 academic year. We can provide, however, some theories based on our knowledge of the schools and the data we collected. One theory is about the availability and prestige of calculus. Another theory is about peer competition, particularly competing as young women against young men.

The Availability and Prestige of Calculus

When St. Elizabeth's adopted the Chicago Series, the decision to discontinue calculus proved to be the most troubling aspect of converting to the new curriculum. It was also the most controversial. For decades, calculus had been the carrot dangling at the end of the secondary mathematics curriculum. Most American high schools still consider it a source of pride and achievement to offer calculus. Among college preparatory schools, it is practically a condition of membership.[7] The admissions literature from such schools frequently mentions statistics about the number of students sitting for Advanced Placement Exams and their success rate. By discontinuing calculus, St. Elizabeth's set itself apart from other college preparatory schools – purposefully charting a curricular course quite different from its peers – in the interest of offering the "best" possible education for girls.

It was never clear what was meant by "best": that the young women would like math and want to learn more? that their mathematical knowledge would increase? that they would enroll in more mathematics courses? get better grades? score higher on standardized tests? or that they would have a more positive classroom experience with increased opportunities to construct their own meanings? While St. Elizabeth's administrators and faculty may have intended all of those improvements, in reality, without calculus in the curriculum, students had less to aspire to in mathematics. The St. Elizabeth's math program proved to be ahead of its time. Because of the role that calculus continues to play in universities and St. Elizabeth's desire to remain a college preparatory school, calculus was restored as the capstone of the math curriculum in fall, 1998.

Young Women Competing with Young Men

As we analyzed math achievement data for female students, Grove's consistent exceptional performance warranted explanation. St. Elizabeth's had a reputation for attracting stronger students than Grove, although comparison of 8th grade records indicated no significant variation between the two groups. Why were the young women at Grove showing more affinity and ability for mathematics? We can only speculate. But we do know that the graduating 1994 class, the last all-female class at Grove, reluctantly welcomed young men to their school. In our conversations with those senior women, they expressed a desire to prove themselves to their male classmates. Down the road, at Xavier, we heard similar sentiments from the newly arriving young women. They wanted to prove themselves to be just as capable or more capable than their male peers. In both instances, the female students were not simply competing for academic recognition, they were competing as young women against young men. They seemed to understand that their performance would define their sex in the emerging coeducational climate. At St. Elizabeth's, academic choices and outcomes did not have the same gendered meaning. Dropping math simply meant there would be fewer students in the class, not fewer females achieving in comparison to males. Under conditions of female–male comparison, the Grove young women had more to prove. Having experienced their school as an all-female institution, they wanted people to recognize that St. Theresa of the Grove had served its students well.

Our theories do not deny other factors contributed to the math achievement outcomes of the young women in this study, such as prior math experiences and teacher quality. However, we believe the absence of the referent other, in this case males, played a notable role in the mathematical experiences of the young women at St. Elizabeth's. In both coeducational settings, young women showed signs of forming structures of solidarity that enabled them to compete in what has traditionally been a man's game – mathematics. The math faculty at St. Elizabeth's were trying to create a new game or at least change the fundamentals of an old game. We happened upon St. Elizabeth's in the initial years of its efforts, when the rules were still unclear.

Outside the brick walls of St. Elizabeth's, however, the public perceptions of mathematics remained relatively unchanged. Internally, the St. Elizabeth's math faculty could redefine the discipline and empower students to think mathematically. Yet, they could not alter the external reality – men continue to dominate mathematics. Insulated from this reality, their female students exhibited minimal interest in challenging or attempting to change this reality. In the coeducational environment, on the other hand, the potential for sex-based inequities in mathematics confronted young women directly; and they responded with enhanced energy for learning math and working hard to meet the challenge.

Notes

1   All data for this chapter were collected solely by Kasi Allen Fuller in the course of producing her doctoral dissertation, "With boys or without them: An exploratory study of mathematics education for girls in single-sex and coeducational high schools," Stanford University, 1997.

2   In the years since the initial appearance of the Standards, other textbooks involving more hands-on exercises and a more committed constructivist approach have appeared on the market. Such texts generally incorporate the Standards on a whole new level, for example encouraging students to develop their own alternative algorithms as opposed to relying primarily on the traditional ones – something the University of Chicago Series does not do. However, at the time that the faculty at St. Elizabeth's were making their decision, the first edition Chicago Series textbooks represented the forefront of reform in mathematics education from a curricular standpoint.

3   These are taken directly from the 1990 edition of *The University of Chicago Mathematics Project Advanced Algebra* textbook, Scott, Foresman publishers.

4   One of the reasons St. Elizabeth's chose this strategy was the faculty's belief that older students encountering the books midway through their high school careers would find the books too radically different from those to which they were well accustomed. A fourth Catholic high school in the area also tried the Chicago Series during this same period. However, the implementation process was more immediate than the plan employed by St. Elizabeth's; and after considerable difficulty, the faculty chose to continue the book only at the algebra II level.

5   The process of selecting textbooks at each of the schools reflected a great deal about larger differences with respect to departmental decision making. St. Elizabeth's is the only department that changed books by consensus – it is a department-wide decision. At the other two schools, such decisions seemed to be either handed down from a department chair or administrator, or made on a more individual basis.

6   It is curious that these two men were also the only men in the study who at one point in their career had taught in an all-female school.

7   It is quite common for high schools both public and private (particularly those that identify as college preparatory) to offer small sections of calculus at a financial loss, simply so that they can include the prestigious course among their list of offerings.

6   Action Research and Feminism

Our study began with Xavier Preparatory High School seeking our help with action research; administrators wanted useful data for preparing for the entrance of young women and the effects of their presence on the heretofore all-male learning environment. At the same time, two other high schools wanted to understand the change to coeducation because they would be affected significantly. With two high schools making a change to coeducation and the third affirming its commitment to all-female education, we thought we could provide practical help. Above all, we wanted to seize this unique research opportunity to learn more about gender in single-sex and coeducational schools.

In the early stages we, seven researchers, recognized that while we shared an ill-defined feminist perspective, there was no time to explore what our varied understandings of feminism meant for our work; we simply thrust ourselves, as did the practitioners, into collaboration with energy and enthusiasm. We did all believe in the power of action research to make a difference in the schools. Also, we shared with the administrators and teachers on the planning team, the hope that valid data would improve the decision making of the schools' staff and faculties. But, once the research was underway, many Xavier administrators and faculty seemed reluctant to spend additional time on study and reflection; they wanted to get on with the transition.

When we undertook the study we did not consider the challenges and difficulties of trying to collaborate, develop an action research agenda, or how our feminist perspective would affect the course of events. We also did not anticipate how the action research would intellectually change us or cause us to reconsider our idiosyncratic ways of being or knowing. We discovered, however, as feminist scholar Shulamit Reinharz (1992) pointed out in her review of feminist action research, that "although changing the researcher is not a common intention in feminist research, it is a common consequence" (p. 194).

This study did teach and change each of us. We learned first hand about the concepts that became the subsequent cognitive framework for our analysis of gender consciousness and privilege, and how they frame experiences of school community members. We learned that although conducting feminist, school-based action research might give rise to deep reflection and responsive action, it might simultaneously introduce difficulties and problems that threaten its effective implementation. We learned how studying gender consciousness and privilege can affect collaborative relationships between researchers and the researched. We saw effective work and affective relationships among us seven researchers ebb and flow. We were sobered by how the best intentions of everyone involved may fall short without good communication and shared goals. We reflected long and hard on our intentions and actions. And from those often poignant interactions we changed how we, as action researchers, will work with educators in the future, both in the capacity of staff development and how we collaborate with fellow researchers to improve schooling for young people.

In this chapter we address how our feminist perspectives and actions worked for and against our ability to understand gender consciousness and privilege and to conduct effective school-based action research. Did we live up to our ideals? Did we live up to the principles of action research? To answer those questions, we discuss what it means to promise to conduct action research from a feminist perspective. Knowing that promises can become challenges, we go on to examine critically how studying issues of gender and gender consciousness and privilege can affect collaborations between both the researchers and the researched, and the researchers as well, as we negotiated shared meanings to explain our data. We conclude with suggestions for how action research can address school-based issues raised through our examination and recommend ways to conduct action research to reach negotiated, shared meanings.

Themes of Promise

We did not use methods unique to feminist research. We employed qualitative and quantitative methods used generally by social scientists in many types of research. Our feminism was directed toward discovering and examining the hidden gaps, unspoken assumptions, and blank spaces of gender consciousness and privilege. As such, our work focused on three promises of feminist research, that it:

1 combines reflection and action with the goal of improving the world of females;
2 focuses on the understanding of both how gender is constructed and what females experience; and
3 stresses collaboration between the researchers and the researched.

Reflection and Action

Action research from a feminist perspective is based on a constructivist world view, that knowledge is created and not discovered, and that participants' subjective experiences are as "true" as the researcher's observations, or so-called "objectivity." "Praxis," a word frequently used by feminist researchers, means the integration of reflection and action whereby the researchers and the researched come together to reflect upon emerging findings and to act upon them (Hollingsworth, 1994; Lather, 1991). The data of reflection become practical for action. As a result, the nature of what is being studied often changes.

Praxis-oriented research calls for researchers and the researched to negotiate meanings and interpretations interactively that "invites reciprocal reflexivity and critique" (Lather, 1991, p. 59). We negotiated meaning with the members of the planning committee using several methods including: (1) member checking (Lincoln and Guba, 1985), a process of clarifying and validating data in follow-up interviews and focus groups, and (2) sequential, interactive interviews that were mutually educative and self-disclosing (Lather, 1991). We found that linking reflection and action encouraged all participants to talk about the data in ways that reached deeper understandings while unmasking the invisibility and listening to the silences of gender assumptions and privilege.

Experience of Females

Feminist research focuses on females' experiences and the conditions that might lead to positive changes in their world (Harding, 1987; Lather, 1991). It assumes a starting point of endemic patriarchy; patriarchy means a normatively accepted power relationship between males and females that awards males unearned privilege.[1] Patriarchy rests on the conceptual meaning given to gender; that is, the social attribution generally given to an individual based on sex. Patriarchy, as we define it, is embedded in the social structures of society and is institutional and not necessarily a part of the personal intentions of individuals. Thus, individual men or even groups of men are not necessarily the problem females face. Rather, females' restricted social and life choices rest in the structured and normatively accepted power relationships that, whether anyone wants it or not, give males unearned privileges and advantages that females do not have. The problem is sustained by the fact that many males and females accept this condition, and do not work to change it.

Focusing on the female experience can make visible the privileges and power relationships of endemic patriarchy; one way people seem to understand privilege is when they do not have it. Thus, we held year-long focus-group conversations with female students, collected data about teacher–student interactions, and focused on the female experience in class-rooms.

Collaboration

Feminist researchers such as Patti Lather (1991) and Sandra Hollingsworth (1994) have made a direct connection between feminist methodology and collaboration. In our collaborative action research project we conceptually rejected the traditional empirical stance of researchers as "expert" and school people as "subjects." We eschewed the hierarchical distinction between researchers and practitioners, believing that the educators in the three schools were as important as story tellers and theoreticians as were we, the researchers. As our data were being refined through dialogue and reflection between the practitioners and ourselves, we became the "subjects" of study in the reciprocal give and take of data examination and interpretation of meaning.

We wanted to use the participants' experience as a path to understand their world and for the development of useful theory. Thus, we developed "planned conversations" which were structured conversations between the researchers and study participants (Hollingsworth, 1994). Our two-way conversations usually began with one of us giving the data and interpreting them, indicating her observations or her interpretation of events. The practitioner or student then gave her/his interpretation of the same data so that we could negotiate clarity, and come to some agreement about our differing understandings.

Through our emphases on research as praxis, the centrality of the female experience, and democratic collaboration, we hoped to create knowledge useful to scholars and to practitioners. We sought to make the data useful to teachers, administrators, and students in the three schools; we hoped to provide formative data that would give them ideas to create healthy learning environments. We especially wanted to clarify how school participants construct gendered meanings for students so educators could use that information to improve the condition for females in schools. We believe we did uncover some silences and invisibilities of gender bias and privilege and, through our conversations and feedback, helped some teachers make some appropriate alterations. Unfortunately, the challenges that arose from our trying to proffer a feminist lens when many administrators and teachers were not ready or wanting to look through it, along with the time-consuming complexities of collaborative, action research, threatened the reciprocal learning and continuing dialogue we had hoped would develop.

The Challenges

The primary goal of action research is to stimulate reflection and action, while the primary goal of classroom instruction is to help students learn the curriculum and to achieve academically. While these goals may appear fundamentally different they can be complementary and should serve each other in creating better schools. Teachers often conduct their own action research to improve their classroom environments (Schmuck, 1997). But anyone who has worked in schools knows that teachers have too little time, feel overloaded, find difficulty in scheduling meetings and dealing with multiple daily demands; all of which conspire against a collaborative action research agenda. Although both action research and classroom instruction are concerned with doing the right thing (Wong, 1995), those conflicting purposes were our greatest challenges and led to worries that we were not being helpful.

very important [handwritten margin note]

In the following section we focus on two areas:

1   ethical and relational responsibilities, and
2   collaborative interpretive processes.

Ethical and Relational Responsibilities

We began this action research project with a bias. We believed from the onset that we might not be bearers of "good news." Our experience with feminist issues in schools caused us to doubt that a change to coeducation would result in an educational environment that benefited young women in the same way it benefited young men. For instance, we started by predicting to the school principal of Xavier that "Xavier won't look any different in five years excepting for having young women in classrooms or hallways." Our feminist research task was to describe the changes that occurred when Xavier became coeducational, and what would be the consequences for Xavier young women and young men as well as for the faculty members.

We were committed to collaborative procedures of gathering data, reflection, dialogue, and reciprocal give and take that called for conducting research "with," but not "on," the school participants. We wanted to develop a common and shared language to interpret data, and to have sufficient time to access the knowledge and understandings garnered. While those commitments are not unique to feminist thinking, failure to live up to any of them is a perennial concern in action research. For us in this project, we wanted especially to examine our successes and failures in keeping those commitments because of our ethical responsibilities to be true to our feminist philosophies and beliefs and to our wish to build trusting relationships with the school participants. We continually asked ourselves: What are the ethics and moral values of the researcher–educator relationship? How do we, as researchers, maintain honesty with the school participants? How do we discuss sensitive issues such as power differentials and different understandings about what is happening during change? How do we deal with different

123

philosophies of knowledge? We intended this research to be *with* rather than *on* teachers. We were not successful. We wanted to redefine the traditional role of expert researcher to that of change facilitator, but we found that administrators and teachers did not accept us in that new role. We succumbed to the demands of time and other challenges described in the following sections, thus we did not sustain the dialogue necessary to build mutual trust and to create a language of common discourse.

Conflicting purposes

"I'm glad you are here to help us figure out how to make this a good school for young women" was the sentiment of most Xavier teachers and administrators at the beginning of our study. We wanted to help them; we wanted to see them create a good school for young women. As the research continued, however, our early mutual purpose began to fade away. They wanted concrete advice and recommendations; we wanted dialogue. They wanted answers; we asked questions. As the research progressed they found they were not getting the advice and answers they sought. When we did give specific answers or advice, most of them chose to eschew them. As the research progressed, our purposes became further and further apart.

The purpose of educators is to organize a school for students to learn effectively; they have to deal with curriculum, staff meetings, student attendance and absences, sports events, dances, assemblies, discipline, class schedules, and grading. Students attend school to earn a diploma, to be with friends, to learn subject areas, to participate in extra-curricular activities, and to proceed onto the next stage of their lives. Educators and students live and interpret their school lives through multiple lenses of roles, emotions, and personal life dilemmas. Our purpose, as researchers, is to narrow our focus – to collect data and inspire reflection and action on a particular topic – in this case, the effects of coeducation on young women. (Gradually we realized we were studying the effects of coeducation on both young women and young men.)

Balancing time demands of action research with school life

"Can't make the meeting after school – I have to meet with a parent." "Sorry, the staff cannot take another meeting – we are just 'meetinged out.'" Collaborative research requires time; it takes time to have conversations, to have meetings, to solve problems, and to reach mutual understandings. The dilemma of time became most apparent when the researchers' and educators' purposes were no longer clearly aligned. A year after boys entered the freshman class at Grove, and after the first term of the change to coeducation at Xavier, we heard comments such as: "I think we're doing just fine don't you?" "I don't think we'll need any more assistance – I think we're meeting our objectives." "Why are we still talking about it – let's just do it?"

During the first semester of our research, the research team members put in approximately 200 hours over and above their regular full-time jobs, the teachers and administrators on the planning committee each devoted at least twenty hours in meetings with the research team. Xavier teachers spent from four to forty hours over the year depending on how involved they were with the research, and some students spent two hours monthly in student focus groups. It became evident that the lack of financial support for release time for the educators and researchers was a problem, creating a burden and a constant source of frustration for everyone.

After the change to coeducation at Xavier, we reminded ourselves that people go through a developmental sequence in an innovation; initially consciousness is high about the innovation and finally, if the innovation "takes," the process becomes "institutionalized" or "the way we do business around here"; no one thinks about it anymore (Fullan, 1991). Psychologically, people cannot live continuously on the precipitous edge of change; they either institutionalize it or the change fades away. We worked with the staffs of the three schools when their consciousness about gender was visible, acute, and urgent; Xavier wanted to do a good job in educating females, St. Elizabeth's feared lowered enrollment if females chose Xavier, and Grove wanted to attract boys so enrollments would remain stable.

Once coeducational classes were in place at Xavier and Grove and it was clear St. Elizabeth's was not in economic jeopardy, it looked like "business as usual" in each school. The faculty and administration grew tired of our questions, tired of our probes, and wanted to "just do it." Their need for creative solutions did not match our need for valid data and our reciprocity was diminished.[2]

Creating a language of common discourse

"What have you learned?" "What should we do differently?" "Are we doing OK?" Educators asked questions like these during the first year of our collaboration. Teachers and administrators wanted us to confirm they were doing okay; they wanted information about what they could do better so long as our recommendations fit their expectations and hopes. They were concerned with the success of their work with students. We, on the other hand, raised questions such as: "What do you see as the meaning of that event?" "Is there a hidden curriculum?" "What are the messages communicated by the school mascot?" Words such as "embeddedness," "privilege," "gendered institutions," "constructivist learning," "deconstruction," and "feminism" were in our research lexicon and fell easily from our researcher lips; perhaps they thought our questions and our words were irrelevant to their work.

As we worked through the second year, it became clear our conflicting purposes and insufficient time were exacerbated by the vocabulary of our discourse. We did not share the same discourse; this is a problem common to educators and researchers. The word "discourse" is a case in point. Discourse signals an institutional way of talking, thinking, and writing. It is a language unique to a profession. Practicing teachers share a discourse; Catholics share another discourse; researchers share still another discourse. By sharing a discourse members of an institution share a common language and a common way of seeing the world. The common discourse of a particular group helps to socialize its members into its special subculture. It affects how group members think and feel about their world.

Time limitations and conflicting purposes kept us from developing a common discourse. As action researchers, we felt ethically obliged to speak in ways that respected the educators' experiences, validated what they knew, and helped them analyze ways to improve conditions for their students. Honest reciprocal dialogue is necessary for developing a common discourse. For that to happen, trust must exist between those in dialogue; and trust takes time to build.

Our first test of reciprocal trust took place early in the project when we provided faculty members with survey feedback drawn from the individual interviews. As we noted in Chapter 1, "silences" was a category we developed to characterize our interviews with Xavier faculty. In our search for embedded issues of gender, we asked ourselves: "what were Xavier faculty *not* saying?" To uncover embedded issues and to deconstruct narrative stories, we believed it would be useful to focus on what they were *not* saying as well as what they were saying. Administrators and teachers on the planning team, however, did not share our view; they accurately argued our interpretation of "silences" came out of our feminist bias. Whereas we saw feminism as an intellectual perspective and we sought to use a feminist lens to understand their school, they wanted us to be "objective" observers of their school.

We did not present our "silences" category at that faculty meeting. Unfortunately, the meeting was conducted early in the morning before school and there was no time for dialogue as we had hoped. While we continued to make some presentations at later faculty meetings, and to meet with small groups of educators, or individual teachers, the communication and reciprocal collaborative relationships never developed.

Kasi Allen Fuller, however, continued action research and consulting with St. Elizabeth's, as described in Chapter 5. The rest of us moved away from the role of change facilitator and turned to the writing of this book to create discourse about gender consciousness and privilege in schools. We would, through sustained conversations among ourselves, focus on maintaining a commitment to the educators' and students' narrative stories.

Thus, we repositioned ourselves to use the data and especially the teachers' stories to create the discourse of this book.

Collaborative Interpretive Procedures

Martin says:

> A social scientific perspective is an interpretive framework that is subjectively imposed on the process of collecting and analyzing cultural data. A social scientific perspective is not considered here to be an objective description of empirical facts. That is not because researchers are careless, dishonest or otherwise inadequate social scientists. It is because different researchers, studying the same cultural members and the same organizational events with equal care, skill, and honesty may evaluate, recall, and interpret what happens differently.
>
> (Martin, 1992, p. 12)

Wasser and Bresler (1996) noted that feminist research offers a rich source of ideas and theories about making collaborative interpretations. They argued feminist research informs us "that different ways of constructing knowledge produce different kinds of knowledge and raising the inescapable question: How does gender – and other significant historical, political, or social features – leave its stamp on the processes and products of a group's interpretation?" (pp. 6–7).

There is never one version of an event, even when we are all present throughout the event. And there is always a danger when we try to uncover "multiple meanings"; we may create a revision that is a new, fictionalized version. Narrative inquiry allowed us to integrate the many and different stories we heard, and rearrange them in presenting our meanings and interpretations (Casey, 1996). The following story illustrates one of many narratives we revisited throughout our work. New information and deepened understandings were mined with each visit.

The St. Elizabeth's story

When we began our study we knew St. Elizabeth's had decided to remain single-sex. What we didn't know at the time was the significant role played by St. Elizabeth's principal in Xavier's decision to become coeducational in five years instead of their plunging quickly ahead. Xavier's decision to move to coeducation could have adversely affected St. Elizabeth's enrollment because both schools educated children from the same families and drew from the same clients in the Catholic diocese. Although Xavier had autonomy to make its own decision with its religious and patriarchal privilege, the St. Elizabeth's principal was successful in raising the issue to the diocese level; this required collaboration and joint problem solving of all Catholic schools in the diocese. Her efforts resulted in the diocesan bishop prevailing on Xavier to take five years for the transition to coeducation, thereby allowing St. Elizabeth's to find its niche and craft a singular mission to educate young women. The power of male privilege and its effects might have gone unquestioned had it not been for the intervention of St. Elizabeth's principal.

The successful action of St. Elizabeth's principal in insisting that Xavier be accountable to the larger community and its "sister" schools dramatically affected the course of Xavier's transition to coeducation and the outcome for girls' education in the region. We, the researchers, had access to this story, but only came to appreciate its impact when we revisited the question, "What makes St. Elizabeth's a feminist environment? It wasn't always like this." Then we could understand the evolution of St. Elizabeth's as a uniquely all-female school.

Feminist Research: Presenting a Plurality of Views of Truth

When describing our research project to someone, a usual response is, "What an interesting project – and what did you find out?" Group member Patricia Schmuck told us that she is:

> always "stuck" for an answer and I mumble something out about "gender privilege and consciousness," which, I am sure, means little to the questioner. Why am I "stuck" with such a question? Why should I be surprised at the question? The purpose of science, from a traditional positivist view, has been to research, identify, simplify and conclude. "What did you find out?" is a reasonable question. But I cannot find a reasonable answer.
>
> (Schmuck et al., 1996, p. 8)

The purpose of feminist research, in contrast to traditional positivist science, is not to simplify, or to objectify, or to be value free, nor is it to determine a fixed single natural reality. Feminist researchers instead adopt a postmodern view of multiple realities; we try to take a snapshot of a rich and varied reality that is in constant change. Ruth Bieler (1984) in her book, *Science and Gender*, explained:

> It follows that no single individual scientist, scholar, or theorizer can produce the "whole truth" about a given phenomenon. Each of us brings to the inquiry, to the investigation of a particular phenomenon, our own life history of experiences, knowledge and attitudes as well as our particular skills and training, and, consequently each illuminates one or another facet of the complex phenomenon we are trying to

explain. Together we illuminate many different facets, all varied aspects of the "truth." It is through this plurality of shared views and voices that we come to some understanding of nature, society, and ourselves.

(p. 201)

The seven of us aspired toward a "plurality of shared views and voices" to present a varied truth of an all-male high school becoming coeducational. This is, however, an objective easier to describe than accomplish.

We observed, analyzed, evaluated, and interpreted our school data from our position as feminist researchers; we looked through the lens of gender and explored the female experience as our guiding focus. The administrators, teachers, and students in the three schools might, of course, interpret the data differently. They have a different lens and different focus. That is not to say one of us is right and the other is wrong. But the challenge of creating a common purpose between educators who are in the business of running a school and feminists who are intent on consciously using their research data to help teachers and administrators change the school environment remained formidable.

Learning the Lessons

We did not achieve the degree of reciprocal learning we had sought with our educator colleagues in the three schools we studied. What would we do differently? We offer the following as recommendations for future work on gender to ourselves as well as to our readers.

1 Develop a Common Discourse

Getting on the same page with a shared lexicon means both parties must acknowledge the need for two-way reciprocal communication, authentic dialogue, and spending time on trust building. Expectations, assumptions, and theoretical perspectives regarding methodologies, interpretation, and the development of knowledge must be talked about. Structure the research design to include regular opportunities for revisiting these issues because they change as the research progresses. Actively attend to the use of specialized language, understanding that the power of words can include or exclude as well as make central or marginalize.

2 Expect Conflicting Purposes as a Function of Prior Experiences

Embrace conflict between practitioners and researchers with the understanding that it can be highly productive.

> Substantive conflict during collaboration is not only normal, but also can be productive, in large part because it gives collaborators more time to generate and critically examine alternatives and to voice disagreements on their way to making a decision.
>
> (Burnett and Ewald, 1994, p. 22)

Educators may not recognize the democratic principles of researchers and may not think of themselves as equal partners in the action research. Most school-based research in the past has been traditional, with the outsiders (researchers) conducting research on the insiders. Relationships are also influenced by factors such as expertise, personality, and the nature of the research project (Hafernik et al., 1997). Relationship differences between researcher and practitioner are exacerbated by differences in language and respective purposes. Use the tension and the conflict to achieve higher levels of understanding and awareness for both researchers and the researched.

3 Acknowledge the Inherent Tension Between Action Research as Knowledge Production and Action Research as a Form of Staff Development

For action research as knowledge production, participants must keep the idea of new knowledge continually before them and they must talk regularly about the following questions: Whose knowledge is it? Who will present it? What form will it take? And who will benefit? For action research as staff development, the participants must keep concerns about power before them. Who is being developed? By whom? In whose interests? How can power be shared? Most action research offers "the possibility of changes that address not the legitimating of practices structured by existing conditions of schooling but the transformation of education through continuing thought and action" (Noffke, 1997, p. 334).

4 Take Time for Reflection on Action

The commitment to reflection, action, and critique is not limited to raising research questions and to building relationships between researchers and research participants. The commitment must also be acted upon by research team members as they learn from the data and negotiate the meaning of the data among themselves. We agree with Patti Lather who argued research is feminist only if it is linked to action; the data of research should help participants understand and change their situations (Reinharz, 1992, p. 75).

5 *Address the Ethical and Relational Responsibilities of Feminist Research*

When researchers embrace feminist ideals, they commit themselves to attend to the relationships between themselves and the practitioners. Feminist researchers must define an ethic of fidelity and care up front and make commitments to hold true to that ethic (Schulz et al., 1997). It is ultimately the researchers' responsibility to uphold the ideals of feminist research despite conflicts of purpose, limitations of time, and differences of discourse that arise. This acknowledges the power and privilege of our researcher position and our moral duty to mitigate our power and privilege through fidelity and care.

6 *Bring a Framework for Understanding Gender to the Faculty, as Early as Possible*

Although the gender consciousness and privilege framework developed as our study emerged, it might have been helpful to have presented those ideas to the faculty at the beginning of the study. Faculty members then might have been clear about what we were thinking, and accept or reject our ideas.

From one point of view, the research purposes of our study were fulfilled: we developed a gender consciousness and privilege framework gathered directly from daily events in the schools, interviews, and surveys. But even a tentative and undeveloped shared framework could help researchers and educators develop mutually through continuing dialogue and creating a common discourse. The gender framework, at best, proffers a model which participants and researchers can push against, argue for, or test out. Ultimately, it should support continuing dialogue and help to create a common discourse understood by all.

Notes

1　Patriarchy generally refers to "white male dominance." While minority men do not have the privilege of Caucasian men, within each race and ethnic group females face more restrictions and lack of choices than their male counterparts (Collins, 1990).

2　Interestingly, students were still eager and willing to talk with us, perhaps because the topic was of interest to them psychologically and developmentally, not because they were interested in its organizational manifestations. In fact, Xavier male students objected to us working with a group of female students; the males wanted their voices heard also. Consequently, we conducted two male student focus groups near the end of the first year of coeducation.

7 Conclusions

In this research we examined the effects that society's collective consciousness about gender and its unspoken assumptions about male privilege have on school learning environments. We examined how the culture of the school organization shapes experiences of all participants, students and faculty alike. In this chapter we (1) summarize our findings in order to build a framework for understanding the gendered nature of school organizational environments; (2) consider gender consciousness and privilege on a continuum as a means for assessing how equitable school environments are; and (3) offer several policy implications for school administrators and teachers to consider.

The Gender Consciousness and Privilege Environment

Figure 7.1 summarizes the interaction of variables at work in a school environment that affect an individual's actions and an organization's culture about gender consciousness. Gender consciousness is contextual, developing, changing, and dependent on social context, school culture, teachers' and staff's beliefs and student backgrounds, understandings and perceptions. The four positions we describe – unexamined thoughts and behaviors, sex equity, gender awareness, and critical transformation – are simply markers or indicators along an infinite number of positions toward increased understanding of the meaning of gender and privilege, and a more developed consciousness about the relationship between the two. We can only surmise what education from a critical transformative orientation would look like (see Figure 7.1); we saw very few indications of it in the schools we studied. Feminist theory, critical theory, visionary individuals, and experiences in other schools where there is an active struggle to change personal actions and organizational life, provide glimpses into unfolding possibilities that may some day become part of the prevailing gender consciousness.

The construct, gender consciousness, focuses on actors' intentions and behaviors. Privilege exists within all environments and influences the actors'

Figure 7.1 The Gender Consciousness and Privilege Learning Environment: A Framework for Education

The Gender Consciousness – Privilege Learning Environment:
A Framework for Education

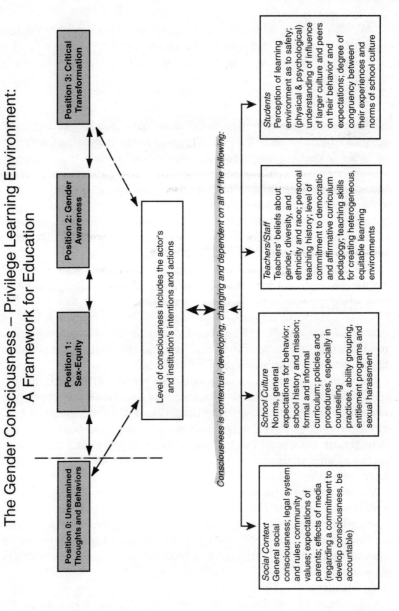

intentions whether or not they are aware of its influence. Actors' intentions and behaviors interact and coalesce to form the cultural milieu – the symbols, actions, norms, and values that form the internal context of organizational settings.

Lisa Delpit (1995) wrote:

> We all interpret behaviors, information and situations through our own cultural lenses; these lenses operate involuntarily, below the level of conscious awareness, making it seem that our own view is simply "the way it is."

(p. 151)

Intention is an especially important part of the cultural lens we used in this study for understanding gender. While a teacher may *intend* to act in sex-equitable or gender-aware ways, students may actually experience certain practices as sex or gender biased, given their own cultural expectations and perceptions of what is fair and equitable. The reverse may also be true: the privileged practices associated with gendered expectations may be so ingrained within cultural norms that students or teachers may not even perceive those practices as sex or gender biased. How can one see the invisible? How can one make the familiar strange?

Privilege and gender are normative filters through which assumptions about reality are made and maintained, effectively excluding some people from opportunities and chances to be heard (Bohmer and Briggs, 1991). Rusch and Marshall (1995), in their review of literature about school administrators, wrote that "deeply embedded gender filters function to maintain the privilege of dominant white-male culture by silencing ideas and people that might disrupt the privilege of dominance" (p. 2).

Privilege complicates constructions of gender within an organization since privilege is not readily discerned by individuals, precisely because everyone is *subject* to it, that is, embedded in it. Privilege does not become a visible, or obvious *object* to its beholders, until individuals or groups become more gender conscious; one's recognition of privilege and the influences it has on gender affects the position one holds on the gender-consciousness continuum.

We saw the dialectic between privilege and gender within the schools we studied in two ways: (1) the unquestioned primacy of the male and the effects that patriarchy have in casting fundamental assumptions about what is valued and what is not valued in a school, and (2) the privilege of elite schools, which fosters unquestioned assumptions about the reproduction of knowledge.

The Primacy of the Male

Social Context

Societal institutions, classroom teachers, and students operate within gendered milieus where the privilege of the male affects culture, organizational structures, and actions. Our story began with Xavier's plans to change from an all-male to a coeducational school with little concern for the effect of its decision on its sister schools. Xavier's power and privilege – being a Jesuit school in the Catholic, male-dominated hierarchy conferred special status – meant that it would have carried out its original plan but for the persistence and objections of the principal of St. Elizabeth's Academy. St. Elizabeth's Academy and St. Theresa of the Grove High School, both all-female, successfully pressed their case with the diocese for a regional study that eventually allowed them to forge acceptable organizational responses to Xavier's proposal. They were able to curb Xavier's unquestioned power and avoid potentially disastrous consequences by exerting a call to conscience within the closely knit Catholic community (Feeney, 1997). Both schools faced the possibility of severe losses in enrollments and possible closure if they remained all-female high schools.

The post-Title IX era proved a powerful social context; the emphasis on sex equity (as defined by providing same opportunities) coupled with current economic realities influenced St. Theresa of the Grove High School to change from an all-female school to coeducation, and it created a new, less feminine, more "neutral" name, Grove Catholic High School, so it would not be so singularly associated with females and its all-female history. Grove administrators believed that boys would not be attracted to a school with a female name. Unlike Grove, St. Elizabeth's reasserted its mission to educate young women.

The larger social context within which the three high schools decided to change or not to coeducation was the post-Title-IX era. In that context, most educators believed that the best policy for achieving or creating equitable learning environments was to be gender neutral. Gender neutrality was expressed differently, however, in the two schools becoming coeducational. Whereas, Xavier tried to make its curriculum and instruction gender neutral by eliminating sex-biased language and behaviors as a way to make a favorable learning environment for young women, Grove sought to eradicate remnants of the all-female school that it believed would offend or turn away male students.

School Culture

At each school, culture was communicated through the formal and informal norms and general expectations for behavior and provided clear evidence of gendered messages in areas such as the high schools' disciplinary policies and dress codes, curriculum, grouping practices, athletics, extra-curricular activities, informal student relationships, and even policies about sexual harassment. Each school culture emerged through actions influenced by history and mission, communicated through teachers, students, and parents as to academic standards as well as social expectations.

Xavier was known for its prestigious, well-developed, and cohesive culture and it was no surprise that one of the most important committees preparing for coeducation was the parent–teacher committee responsible for redefining the dress code and student conduct. It worked diligently to eliminate references to males, to create neutral language, and to consider consequences of a formerly harsh formal and informal disciplinary policy on young women. And, in a culture where athletics was a defining criterion for leadership and excellence, the faculty and staff were generally proud that they had worked to create similar athletic opportunities for the young women entering Xavier.

Two aspects of school culture, the self-selection factor in perpetuating cohesive and prestigious cultures, and sexual harassment policies, are useful examples of the interplay of gender and culture.

The self-selection factor

School culture had a noticeable effect on student self-selection into Xavier and St. Elizabeth's. The newly arriving young women chose Xavier for its athletics, academic excellence, and family expectations. The new Xavier young women believed that coeducation was the "real world" and that their new school would prepare them for the kind of prestigious college and careers they were seeking. St. Elizabeth's young women chose their school for its academic excellence as well as its climate which defined each young woman as unique and prided itself as a safe place for females to grow and develop. At St. Elizabeth's, in the absence of boys, girls were able to speak out and be themselves. They preferred the lack of social distractions that would be created by a male presence. St. Elizabeth's teachers encouraged or at least allowed students to talk more freely about the social conditions of women than at the other two schools. It was not surprising given how self-selection works that females' satisfaction with their education was high at both Xavier and St. Elizabeth's. The schools had cohesive cultures and were continually clarifying their respective climates more precisely throughout this period (see Epilogue for more discussion); thus we saw that the girls who chose Xavier and St. Elizabeth's knew what to expect and why they were attending each school.

Awareness about sexual harassment

Most schools today have a policy about sexual harassment for students and faculty. Young women may be at risk in schools with male peers. The latter can be a threat, potential or actual, to the physical or psychological safety of the former. Xavier staff was aware that its school climate was heavily masculine and potentially deleterious to girls. Consequently, it developed a policy about sexual harassment. Some Xavier staff members mourned the likely loss of the "special male energy" in the move to create a more "gender neutral" environment. Still, some Xavier teachers were concerned that harassment would not be seriously addressed. Indeed, no one tolerated overt manifestations of harassment. Still, a few student subgroups, notorious for operating independently of teachers' eyes and ears, continued to act out their sexist attitudes and in certain instances, such as student elections, promoted resistance to selecting young women for school government.

Teacher and Staff Beliefs

Educators can no longer perpetuate exclusionary practices. They are normatively unacceptable and unlawful. Yet we know that what educators believe about similarities or differences between males and females influences how they interact with each. Those who believe females are fundamentally different from males often argue for instruction that meets the needs of females differently than males; or they might strive to organize instruction in ways that compensate for sex differences in order to achieve similar outcomes for girls and boys. Those who believe females and males are more alike than different might develop an instruction that is similar for both. And those who believe that more differences exist within the sexes than between them or that generalizations about one group do not help understand individual differences within any subgroup, might work to create learning environments that build on student strengths while addressing weaknesses, deficiencies, and areas for growth in particular subgroups of students or individuals.

Teachers' beliefs about gender, diversity, class, ethnicity, and race develop through their personal histories. Their beliefs may or may not be supported by the school norms. For instance, Charlene Wilson, the Xavier English teacher, held beliefs that were not supported by the school norms; she was in a marginalized position (Gosetti, 1995). On the other hand Brock Bronson, the Grove mathematics teacher, and Nancy North, the St. Elizabeth's social studies teacher, fit into the school norms; in Mr. Bronson's case by *not* noticing or focusing on sex as a factor in his classroom teaching, and Mrs. North's case by *openly* endorsing femaleness.

Teachers' commitments to the value of democratic and affirmative pedagogy can be just as important as their pedagogical skills in creating heterogeneous, equitable learning environments. The majority of Xavier teachers held similar beliefs about gender and their expressed attitudes were an indicator of their level of consciousness about gender and privilege. Most Xavier teachers sought to create fair environments, but they usually defined simple equity practices as "sex-neutral," or "What is good for boys is good for girls." They focused on the teaching practices typically indicative of an understanding of a sex-equity environment: neutral language, a desire to achieve equal treatment of boys and girls in discipline, and the use of "objective" academic assessment practices that either masked or ignored male–female differences in classroom interaction and female access to classroom discourse. Needless to say, they did not always achieve equity. For instance, in discipline some teachers were perplexed because, what was good for boys was *not* necessarily good for girls or, more precisely, what boys would tolerate was not the same as what girls would tolerate. At Xavier the consciousness about gender was consistent with prevailing American standards about sex equity as defined by Title IX; same is equal and gender consciousness is relatively undeveloped.[1]

In each school teachers were guided by local organizational norms of what was acceptable teaching practice about gender consciousness and privilege. One of the most progressive teachers within St. Elizabeth's, by feminist standards, Mrs. North, could not have taught the world history curriculum in the manner she did if she were teaching in an all-male or even coeducational setting such as Xavier. Conversely, Xavier's consciously feminist teacher, Mrs. Wilson, had not yet learned strategies that allowed her to criticize and alter the male, white privilege of an elite curriculum. Xavier did not consider curriculum change as necessary upon the advent of females; after all, when you already have the best curriculum, why question what it teaches about gender?

Students

Students constitute a critical force in shaping the form that a high school culture takes. Because of their marginality within the adult-dominated culture they are in a unique position to recognize and perhaps actively shape what it means to be "classed and gendered." Proweller (1998) referred to that sort of student behavior as "border work" in the "border zone," the place where adolescent girls, in particular, seek "to exercise control over the conditions of their lives in spite of very real dynamics that have the potential to limit the possibilities" (p. 16) of access to "membership" in activities reserved for white, male and upper-middle-class privilege.

We observed the new, female arrivals to Xavier exert a consciousness about gender that exceeded that of their teachers; for instance, young women, when they felt safe to voice their opinions, expressed dismay at the fact that they were not reading female authors in English classes. Still, these same young women were just as likely not to see how male privilege affected their lives, as evidenced by the female senior who accepted without question the judgment of her male peers that the newly arrived female students had brought down Xavier's academic standards. Xavier students were certainly

Is this the same as other marginalized grps experience? desegregation.

subject to the subtleties of gender bias in many classrooms, but only occasionally did a few female students express their negative feelings to an understanding female teacher. More often the female students participated without complaint in whatever expectations the teacher set.

In some cases, young women became silent in the face of male dominance in class and the teacher's exclusionary practices. Or, as in the case of Brock Bronson's math class at Grove, they were helped to become more assertive and less self-doubting or deprecating. Nevertheless, discriminatory practices were noticed by Grove young women in most settings even though they never directly challenged them. The senior Grove women did voice their concerns several times about being powerless to influence sex-biased practices that were introduced under the guise of making the newly arriving young men feel welcome in their school. Their voices did not seem to be heard by most faculty members.

Students' consciousness about gender arises in many ways from their perceptions of the physical and emotional safety of the learning environment, peer expectations about sex appropriate behavior, social constructions of gender in the curriculum, and their own experiences in classrooms and the school culture. Especially in high school where students are struggling through the trials and tribulations of leaving adolescence and entering adulthood, their struggle for self-identity as a female or male is paramount. Students will do their own "border work," quietly forging avenues for self-expression through peer relations and particular school subcultures (Proweller, 1998). When the school offers a safe, secure place and the faculty invites such gender exploration, students may develop a deeper understanding of gender consciousness and privilege as compared to an unsafe school in which the faculty does not permit such conscious work.

Privilege and Unquestioned Assumptions About the Reproduction of Knowledge

We found few teachers with the pedagogical knowledge to correct uneven classroom interaction patterns. Teachers were not aware of how their statements and questions engaged some students more than others. But more importantly, how teachers, administrators, and even students thought about the reproduction of knowledge gave us a more poignant understanding of how privilege in elite schools fosters unquestioned gender-constructed assumptions and values. Topics for study, research, and debate, the actual primary and secondary sources of information encouraged for use and available through the library, and even the inquiry procedures within a particular discipline are subject to gendered constructions and understandings. Privilege, however it is constructed, defines and maintains assumptions, effectively excluding certain ideas and even the value of certain lines of inquiry.

139

At St. Elizabeth's feminist views had already had time to take root through the informal curriculum as evidenced in Mrs. North's class. The faculty's desire to adopt the NCTM standards in mathematics was indicative of a willingness to take a risk on behalf of the young women, a move very few American high schools have yet to take. The faculty and administration of St. Elizabeth's believed that in an all-female environment, they could question the value and status that mathematics holds in this culture, while maintaining acceptable and rigorous standards. The St. Elizabeth's faculty considered itself subject to the same pressures as the Xavier faculty; but its all-female identity may have given it permission to experiment more. In Chapter 5, we noted that formal change in the mathematics curricular sequence did not produce the results St. Elizabeth's hoped for in higher levels of mathematical achievement by a greater number of girls. Counseling and scheduling practices and other informal school norms worked together to reduce the number of "average" girls who exceeded the minimum school requirement in mathematics. At Xavier and at Grove, more girls were taking advanced math courses compared to the numbers of girls at St. Elizabeth's.

The Gender Consciousness–Privilege Continuum

We created the Gender Consciousness–Privilege Continuum as we worked with data about the similarities and differences in gender assumptions and practices from the three high schools. We wondered why most Xavier faculty, in particular, seemed to plateau at the level of sex neutrality – in intention as well as action – as their way for dealing with coeducation. In working with these high schools, we realized teachers needed and wanted a gauge to consider where they were developmentally in creating equitable classroom environments. As we dealt with the data we found that we, too, were limited by our "Title IX thinking" and the concepts of sex equity. As we discussed in Chapter 6, our inattention to sound discourse got in the way of enacting the role of change facilitator in helping faculty members move beyond their current levels of gender thinking. We learned, too, that educators attempting to create sex-same or sex-neutral learning environments was not sufficient for dealing with the concepts of gender consciousness and privilege. Their strategies typically ignored issues of male power and privilege. So how do we move forward?

Fortunately other feminist writers such as Patti Lather (1991), Kathleen Weiler (1988), Catherine Marshall (1997), Jane Kenway and Sue Willis (1997), Peggy Orenstein (1994), Patricia Murphy and Caroline Gipps (1997), and Claire Hiller (1998) helped us struggle through the data to move beyond conventional thinking. We developed the Gender Consciousness and Privilege schema to make sense of our data and to respond to the questions we first raised:

- What does gender consciousness mean for creating truly equitable learning environments?
- How does the level of gender consciousness affect the culture of schools and the experience of students?

Figure 7.2, The Gender Consciousness and Privilege Continuum describes four positions of increasing awareness about unspoken assumptions undergirding valued status positions in the society: e.g., sex, social class, race, age, and physical (dis)ability. We selected indicators drawn from insights gleaned from our data that assess where an individual or an organization might be positioned.

It is important to keep in mind the difference between teachers' intentions and their actual behaviors in relation to gender consciousness and privilege. Indeed, we found gender-focused intentions to be quite discrepant. A few Xavier teachers who articulated a well-developed commitment, and even a rhetorical passion indicative of gender awareness, were hard pressed to take proactive actions to actualize these intentions. They did not have the pedagogical skill nor were they willing to deviate from traditional Xavier norms and to place themselves on the margin of the school culture. Individuals and organizations can be assessed on the continuum by using both intentions and behaviors. Indeed, doing that helps surface contradictions that all people experience between what they think and how they act.

Position 0: Unexamined Thoughts and Behaviors: The Reason for Title IX

The rise of the second feminist movement in the United States brought fuel and passion to an evolving common awareness of sex discrimination in all aspects of society. After the attacks on racism in the civil-rights movement, women began to analyze their own position in society and to organize an attack on sexism. In the turbulent 1960s women's groups began to form even as society's focus was still race. In 1961 President Kennedy established a national commission on the Status of Women, and The National Organization for Women was established in 1966. Many of those newly formed groups focused on education, from the personal recognition of having experienced discrimination and sexism while growing up female in the United States, Australia, Canada, and the United Kingdom. Books such as *Dick and Jane as Victims: Sex Stereotyping in Children's Readers* (Women on Words and Images, 1972) and *Sexism in School and Society* (Frazier and Sadker, 1973) made their rounds, and phrases such as "sex bias," "sex stereotypes," "discrimination," and "sexism" became part of the everyday lexicon. Feminist researchers investigated curriculum, language, teacher interactions, peer relationships, demonstrating to many parents and educators the kinds of intentional and unintentional, overt and subtle practices that made

Figure 7.2 The Gender Consciousness–Privilege Continuum

The Gender Consciousness – Privilege Continuum

Position 0: Unexamined Thoughts and Behaviors

Individuals unquestioningly accept social assumptions and stereotypes for females and males on the basis of sex. Individuals may deny bias and discrimination has occurred for them or for others.

School implements different standards, policies and behavioral consequences for females and males, or the unintended effects of unexamined practices is negative.

Indicators:
- Different treatment and admission standards
- Student activities associated with specific group or another
- Demeaning sexist jokes and remarks
- More attention to the boys/to the girls
- The presence of the other lowers academic standards
- Boys carry/lift – girls clean/set up
- "What's good for boys is good for girls"

Position 1: Sex – Equity

Individuals recognize females and males have been treated differently because of their sex; they make some corrective actions for same treatment.

School changes standards and policies which differentiate on account of sex and provide deliberate compensatory opportunities to redress past inequities on account of sex.

Indicators:
- Standard dress code for males and females
- Equal quality coaches, facilities, sport standards for males and females
- Non-gender specific school profile of the student at graduation
- Uniform counseling and advising

Position 2: Gender Awareness

Individuals recognize same is not always equal and the cultural meanings of being female or male are deeply embedded in thinking and behavior; the concept of sex changes to the concept of gender, recognition of privilege as a factor in equity begins.

School questions the assumptions guiding teaching and learning, curricular choices, extra-curricular activities. The staff looks more deeply into how gender influences classroom teaching and organizational functioning.

Indicators
- Inclusion of greater variety of authors and diversity in English classes
- Increase in non-athletic extra-curricular options for both sexes
- Changed teaching

Position 3: Critical Transformation

Individuals recognize the unspoken assumptions that privilege, which is determined by valued position in the society (sex, social class, race), provides some individuals with access to social rewards.

School helps students question issues of privilege and dominance in the society; the curricula move toward multiple perspectives of reality and encourage questioning how events of the world have been interpreted.

Indicators of Thinking
- Use of gender as a unit of analysis in curricular decision making
- Considers multiple points of view
- God as "He" or "She"
- Invites voices in the margin to name their "position"

school life different for girls than for boys. Despite the thousands of curriculum materials developed and workshops offered during the reform period which followed, however, there are still today many examples of educators with unexamined intentions about females and males in school and who unwittingly perpetuate sexism and sex biases. Position 0 is the place where educators do not see nor do they question the social norms that result in bias or discrimination on the basis of sex, race, or social class. Neither their intentions nor their actions have changed.

Position 1: Sex Equity in Education: The Movement for Reform

In 1997 Americans celebrated the 25th anniversary of the enactment of Title IX of the Educational Amendments of 1972. That law was to produce revolutionary change for young women in education; educators from the United Kingdom, Canada, and Australia also enacted similar legislation around the same time. The language of Title IX is deceptively simple, "No person shall, on the basis of sex, be excluded from participation in, be denied the benefits of, or be subjected to discrimination under any educational program or activity receiving federal funds." The hope was to eliminate institutional bias and discrimination so females could study subjects that would allow them to compete successfully in the sex-segregated marketplace of American society. The focus was on changing institutional obstacles that deter females from freely entering or advancing in all aspects of our society. The underlying ideal holds that all individuals, regardless of attributes, should be free to enter into all walks of society. Individual attributes, such as sex, race, and class, evidently operate to block some people because individuals are segregated in society and within institutions. The Title IX argument is based on the rational belief that *if* institutions were freed of discrimination, individuals would be free to develop their skills based on their interest and their merit. Early on during the implementation of Title IX there was an emphasis on sameness. If girls were to be equal to boys, they should have the same opportunities as boys. But after twenty-five years of its implementation, we have come to realize that "same is not equal"; and that same opportunities do not necessarily provide equal opportunities.

Title IX has made some difference in the lives of young women. The 1970s activists' efforts have paid off to some degree; many educators are more sensitive to sex bias and some institutional practices have changed to improve the lives of females in schools.[2] Some equalizing of female representation in upper-level math and science courses has occurred and test results are showing equal outcomes in the core subject areas (LePore and Warren, 1997; Willingham and Cole, 1997). Change has also occurred in the representation of women in school administration (Schmuck, 1995). But Title IX has not had the revolutionary results hoped for by many activists, partly because of lack of operational policy at state and federal levels, weak enforcement, increasingly conservative court decisions, and the backlash of public opinion (Stromquist, 1997). Title IX enactment emphasized narrow, legal definitions of equality, representing the prevailing thinking of 1972.

We found in our study that the thinking of most educators reflected the best that developed during the Title IX era: i.e., eliminate the differential treatment of females and males in materials, interactions, participation, access to knowledge, and school structures. Differential treatment of males and females has been seen as "unequal"; thus educators are attempting to lessen differential treatment and increase "same" treatment by reducing sex stereotyping, providing more equal access to knowledge, and changing school structures. The goal of the aftermath of Title IX has been the integration of girls into all aspects of the school, paralleling the goals of racial integration. Xavier worked diligently at doing just that.

Position 2: Gender Awareness and Growing Distinctions in the Post-Title IX Era

When Title IX was passed the word "sex" was used to focus the content of the legislation; there shall be no discrimination "on account of sex." Eventually the word "gender" evolved to be used synonymously with "sex" in popular parlance, but for us it is conceptually important to distinguish between "sex" and "gender."

"Sex" refers to one's biology and it is a relatively unchanging category over time; females and males are of different sexes because of their hormonal functioning, physiology, and anatomy. Most of the legislation which developed under Title 1X focused on sex; it compared male opportunities and female opportunities and tried to assure that females will have the same opportunities as males in our educational system.

"Gender," on the other hand, with its emphasis on the social-psychological *meaning* given to being a biological female or biological male, recognizes how behavior associated with and value placed on certain attributes are socially constructed and change over time and from context to context.

In Position 2 educators focus on conflicting viewpoints and different interpretations of the meaning of gender, and locate factors in the environment to explain performance differences between girls and boys. They begin to use privilege as a discriminating idea, and understand the complexity of creating change for equity. An example from a recent research report, "A longitudinal study of gender differences in young children's mathematical thinking," by Fennema et al. (1998) may be useful. The authors reported on a longitudinal study of elementary grades 1–3 where reform ideas in mathematics had been implemented and found that there were, indeed, performance differences between boys and girls on mathematical problem solving in the area that is widely accepted as a predictor of high levels of mathematics achievement in later years. Those results called into question the long-accepted belief that gender differences in math appear first at adolescence. Instead of leaving the reader the task of making sense out of the potentially troublesome findings the editors of *Educational Researcher* invited four interpretative essays from researchers who work from different viewpoints. Judith Sowder (1998), Janet Hyde and Sara Jaffee (1998), and Nel Noddings (1998) each offered a different explanation of the research findings and attempted to locate factors in the environment to explain the performance differences between boys and girls. Sowder, a mathematics teacher, thought that the results indicate important gender differences in learning and suggested that the findings indicate that girls' use of more concrete strategies might lead to less understanding of important ideas on which further learning of mathematics is based. Janet Hyde and Sara Jaffee, social psychologists, thought that the results actually showed minimal differences and that the teachers studied may have unconsciously encouraged stereotypical behaviors which resulted in girls and boys solving problems differently. Nel Noddings, a feminist philosopher, noticed that the findings showed that boys did better on items that emphasized meaning. She wondered whether girls could be less interested in mathematics and how lower interest could lead to lower performance. She lamented also the fact that society did not value as important the cultivation of nurturing qualities in young boys and men in the same way it worried about mathematical performance in girls. In no case, however, in any of these essays was the possibility of essential differences based on biology held as an acceptable reason because such an explanation has no *educational* merit. *This makes no sense*

Understanding the *why* of different performance outcomes has the goal of learning how to better provide teachers the kind of coaching, practice, and instruction that will lead to providing a learning environment better able to support more equal performance outcomes in boys and girls. The gender-aware educator asks, "How should *group* tendencies in terms of research data affect individual choices at one end of the spectrum and policies that support human growth and learning in schools at the other end?" When teachers question assumptions that guide teaching and learning, curricular choices, and extra-curricular activities they look more deeply into how gender influences classroom teaching and school organization functioning, and they realize how embedded gender is in thinking and behavior.

In order to create schools where power is equalized, where marginalized groups can be equal participants and benefit from a positive environment, the gender-aware view of Position 2 must eventually give way to challenging the existing framework of schooling.

Position 3: Critical Transformation

We see critical transformation as a postmodern view; it is a change in how one views the world, a changing *Zeitgeist*, a paradigm shift. The teacher who holds a critical transformative view understands the centrality of privilege in creating position and value for individuals by their attributes. Privilege is always present in society, and it is understood by discerning the relative position of actors or groups in regard to valued attributes. The critical transformative view recognizes the importance of seeing individuals by class, race, gender, and personal history, and concentrates on understanding the experiences of whoever is the marginalized group within the social context. It eschews the romantic view that since we are all human, we are all the same. We are not all playing on a level field because social norms permit some of us more than others to join the game at different levels. Moreover, things are not as they seem, thus events, ideas, and viewpoints need to be "deconstructed" to explore multiple interpretations, and to focus on the power of context (Lather, 1991).

Critical transformation Position 3 emphasizes consciousness about gender and privilege; educators at this point on the continuum are developing emancipatory curricula that focus on the spoken and unspoken assumptions of power distribution and power implementation in the society. The critical transformation view invites discussion about how best to develop educational systems that are good for females and for males, beginning by altering our thinking about the historical primacy and privilege of the white male. Although all white boys are not privileged by class, they carry a sense of ownership of places and events and we saw this many times in the course of our study.

We think that by paying attention to the underlying assumptions about what is "good," we can assist in the reform of educational policy and practice. We do not want to ignore differences and we do not want all students treated the same simply to satisfy the idea that everyone must be treated equally. Teachers and students, however, can become much more aware about how gender consciousness and privilege play out in their own classrooms and schools. They can do something to transform our society.

Single-Sex Education and Public Policy

In our introduction we stated that we were not going to evaluate the schools nor weigh the advantages or disadvantages of single-sex or coeducation. We did learn, however, that all-girl learning environments are acutely at risk in an era of fiscal limitations and that when girls lose their schools they find themselves in schools where policies are put in place to accommodate boys. Or in a school like Xavier, the young women learn to accommodate to the unquestioned assumption that what is good for boys must be good for girls.

An unintended consequence of Title IX is that it disallows experimentation with single-sex classrooms and schools in districts receiving federal funds. Female-only elementary schools and high schools have never been numerous in the American public system; and even before the introduction of Title IX in 1972 most female-only colleges had already become coeducational. Single-sex schooling has been reduced significantly in the private and parochial systems during the last few decades. It is, indeed, ironic that as single-sex schools were being eliminated feminists began questioning whether it was possible to have an equitable education for females in coeducational settings. The argument was that in single-sex schools females can exert their power, express their voice, and assume leadership positions; women are not silenced, stereotyped, or harassed in all-female environments. In 1992, the then Assistant Secretary of Education, Diane Ravitch, convened a group of researchers and practitioners to investigate the condition of single-sex schools. For the first time in over a century the unchallenged ideal of coeducation was being questioned in the United States Department of Education. The preface of the document read:

> The research synthesis produced for this conference and the summary of the conference proceedings suggest that single-sex education provides educational benefits for some students. Clearly, given the limited availability of single-sex education today, very few students will have the opportunity to attend a school for boys, or for girls, or even a single-sex college. The question raised by this study is whether our society should re-examine its received attitudes about single-sex education.
>
> (OERI, 1992, p. 11)

But keeping girls and boys apart does not necessarily provide a good education for either sex. In some all-female high schools Shmurak (1998) found a fundamental lack of gender awareness: the male point of view was continually felt through a curriculum that did not question gender assumptions and counseling practices were stereotypical. Single-sex schools are different one from another, consequently it is not safe to assume that all single-sex schools are places that promote gender consciousness and critique privilege.

The research, at best, is ambiguous and confusing regarding the outcomes and benefits of single-sex schooling. Janice Streitmatter (1998), author of *For girls only: making a case for single-sex schooling*, studied females in single-sex and coeducational schools. She pointed out that some girls' schools use a similar curriculum to what boys' schools use because staff members believe to be different would be less and that would mean to "water down" the curriculum. Even in the all-female setting educators believe that "what is good for boys is good for girls." Other female-only schools were as teacher-directed, text-centered, and traditional in their pedagogy and curriculum as any other school. Streitmatter's all-female schools did little to educate young women in meaningful ways about their public and private roles in society.

Streitmatter also presented some excellent examples of all-female schools, or all-female classes within coeducational schools, that address the unique and special needs of being female in a society. Simply putting girls together, however, does not necessarily provide a better education for them. Parents and educators must consider the individual needs of young women in constructing and selecting learning environments. Certain girls thrived at Xavier given their desire for athletics and their willingness to accept the narrowly normative culture of the school. And, other young women felt that St. Elizabeth's was too sheltered and protective. While public school students do not have a single-sex option, students do respond to different climates and cultures in unique and important ways. Nevertheless, significant differences in school cultures do not mitigate the need to create gender-aware classroom environments everywhere.

We do believe that there are some instances when single-sex experiences are important for females and for males. While it is unlikely that American public school systems will develop single-sex schools, we need more flexibility than allowed under Title IX to experiment with single-sex classes and learning experiences.[3] In any case, educators need to recognize that the work of Title IX has only just begun and that high school environments are gendered organizations. Educators need to do creative work to find innovative ways of making an understanding of gender consciousness and privilege a regular part of staff development, the norms of the organization as well as the school curriculum.

Notes

1   In the interviews Poplin Gosetti (1995) conducted with the faculty and administrators on gender and privilege, she found that at least half of the twelve interviewees could articulate indicators that we define on our continuum at the gender awareness and critical transformation position. Her data point out the difficulties that educators have in making beliefs and intentions congruent with behavior in an organizational context where the culture presents a ceiling for action.

2   For a detailed history of this period and an excellent list of references on the equity issues and educational attainments see Klein and Ortman, 1994.

3   The National Organization for Women along with the New York Civil Liberties Union and a coalition of civil rights groups, filed a complaint in 1998 against the New York City school district to block the all-girls' public school, the Young Women's Leadership School of East Harlem. They argued that the school district discriminated on the basis of sex and violated Title IX, the law they fought so hard for to guarantee equal opportunity. NOW complained that the school should be opened to boys and that if girls are experiencing discrimination in coeducation classrooms, the problem should be confronted where it starts – in coed classrooms (Burk, 1998). The irony is not lost on feminists who recognize that Title IX must be supported and protected, but at the same time our understanding of the questions regarding gender awareness continue to move beyond the legal definitions of sex equity.

Epilogue

It is ten years since Xavier Preparatory's Board of Trustees made the decision to admit young women, ten years since the local archdiocese helped mediate a compromise plan and timetable for the transition to coeducation. It is six years since the first female students actually entered Xavier Preparatory High School. To bring us up to date on what had happened since our last data were collected, we returned to the schools in the spring of 1998, engaging in informal conversations with administrators, students, and parents who had lived through the challenges and changes that accompanied the advent of young women. We especially wanted to learn more about how people view the schools today.

According to what we saw and heard during our visits, all three schools we studied have successfully adapted to the institutional changes (in size, sex composition, mission, and so on) precipitated by the coeducation decision. Xavier has doubled its enrollment to over a 1,000 students; Grove High School, the former all-girls' St. Theresa of the Grove, is coeducational and boasts an enrollment at capacity; St. Elizabeth's Academy continues its strong enrollment and receives awards for its excellence.

A consistent observation across the three schools is the uniquely identifiable culture associated with each one. Looking back, the extended transition time allowed each school to articulate more clearly its purpose and identity. As a result, the larger community can now more easily distinguish the differences between the schools and how each fulfills a particular niche for students. One valuable outcome is less confusion for 8th graders and their families who are trying to match the interests and talents of prospective students with the offerings of the schools.

Returning to the schools also reminded us how much the work of our study, including the focus on gender consciousness and privilege, reflected a particular period in their history – a time when all three schools were working through the consequences of Xavier's decision to become coeducational. Administrators, faculty, students and parents were highly conscious of the sex composition at each school, understandably concerned about what the change might bring. Issues of sex equity were high on everyone's agenda. Now, six years later, the issues of sex equity do not loom as large in our conversations with school participants. The schools have settled into a new pattern that reflects both who they were before as well as the lessons learned from their transition experiences. They are the same and, at the same time, different. All three schools have changed, but much remains unchanged. A look at Xavier best illustrates this paradox.

The physical changes are the first indications of the transformation that has occurred since the admission of young women to Xavier. The stark, utilitarian classrooms and buildings of the campus have been replaced or remodeled into bright, open, and colorful classrooms and learning spaces. New landscaping, artwork, and architectural features grace the campus. Within the classrooms, interviewees also note changes in pedagogy. The traditional teacher-dominated classrooms of the past have given way to classrooms that are more interactive, open, and student-driven. New faculty, recruited and hired during the transition period, possess the skills and philosophical orientation to support a more progressive and egalitarian educational environment.

Xavier has a broader curriculum now than at any time in its history. There are more advanced math, science, and language courses than before. Enrollment figures show relative parity between the sexes among students taking these courses. The arts programs have an enrollment of over 400 students. Remarking on this phenomenon, one Xavier alum noted, "When I was a student here, the art program consisted of the poster club where we would make signs that said 'Beat Central!'."

During the transition to coeducation, Xavier faculty predicted young women would have a "softening" or "civilizing" effect, that their presence would yield a "kinder, more gentle" school culture. These predictions, in a large part, were realized. One administrator noted, "The foundation of Xavier is the religious program. The young women have made fundamental contributions to the religious life at Xavier with their concerned faith life and spiritual commitment." He noted that the young women brought a "humane aspect" which changed the culture at Xavier.

There were some areas, however, where the "softening" phenomenon seemed to have little effect and competition, always a driving force at Xavier, was one of these areas. People we spoke to claim that particularly academic competition has become even more intense in the coeducational environment than it was prior to the transition. Academic benchmarks indicate that the standards are also higher now than ever before. SAT scores have increased every year since 1992 and there is no notable sex distinction in the scores. Valedictorians have been equally male and female. As one interviewee stated, "The girls asked for and received the same opportunities as the boys and have taken and run with it." As before, Xavier continues to attract a particular type of student – male and female – one that thrives in a competitive academic environment.

Several teachers who had been at Xavier during the transition noted that the social relationships between the young men and young women had dramatically changed since the transition year. The "not gender friendly" and "often uncomfortable" interactions observed between male and female students during the transition year have given way to a more "natural relationship" between the sexes. At athletic events, males cheer on the females, females cheer for males. During their junior year, young women returning from the Encounter Retreat are greeted by senior men and share in a celebration Mass together. The sense of community, a hallmark of Xavier, is by all accounts as strong as ever.

Still, student government, reported one administrator, seemed "to be an area that the boys were not able to let go of." For the first four years of coeducation, no young woman was elected to a student body office. Some teachers conjectured that females may have contributed to this disparity by not supporting young women running for office. Today, young women currently occupy about half of the class officer positions and are leaders in clubs such as drama and campus ministry.

In the ten years since Xavier's decision to adopt coeducation, much has changed in the day-to-day details of school life. However, the fundamental characteristics that represent its culture have not changed. Today, Xavier continues to adhere to the values and ideals that have defined the school for decades. The transition to coeducation was not easy for this school. In many ways, the decision to admit women went against the grain of its tradition and culture. But, by making the change to coeducation, the school proved itself capable of the alterations and reconstructions needed to admit young women. Significantly, these changes were made within the parameters of the Jesuit educational tradition. At its core, Xavier remains a Jesuit school.

Changes in institutional practice take time to translate into the culture, curriculum, institutional practice, and student peer culture. With the advent of coeducation, the processes engaged by the Xavier community required them to examine their assumptions, behaviors, and practices related to educating males and females. Xavier's self-conscious examination was a healthy process; it benefited not only young women but also young men.

Today, we see evidence that Xavier continues its self-examination process. The thoughtful, cautious, continuously engaged process of reflection used in the transition has allowed the faculty, administration, and staff to recognize that issues of sex equity were not the only areas the school needed to do work on. Xavier remains an elite school. It attracts students who are academically motivated, athletically talented, generally Caucasian, and largely upper-middle class. We have been told that Xavier would like to become a more inclusive institution. If so, issues of diversity, particularly with respect to ethnicity and socioeconomic status, are among the school's immediate challenges. We recognize that the coeducation experience has increased Xavier's capacity to explore and listen to other voices surrounding issues of inequity. We trust that the school will continue to reflect and self-examine as it proceeds on the path to challenge its historical exclusivity.

Appendix A

Faculty Questionnaire: Xavier High
School, January–February, 1993

-Notes to interviewers:

1   Ask interviewees to sign Human Subject Release Form.
2   Use the standard questionnaire flexibly; make sure all questions are covered, but do not necessarily stick to the order they are asked.
3   Type up responses – as verbatim as possible (use tape back-up if needed).
4   Write up your impressions, how you handled the interview, the flow of questions etc.
5   Probes in questionnaires only to be used as necessary.
6   Push for specific examples.
7   If folks "run on" with answers, stop them, saying there are other questions to answer.
8   Prepare your categories for analysis for meeting, 8:30 a.m., Thursday, February 18 at Xavier High School.

1   Introduce self and the project. Xavier High School is in a unique situation moving from all-boys to a coeducational school. There are a team of people from several universities interested in studying the process you are going through. There will be a number of different research projects going on which will be fully described to you at a later meeting. In this interview we are interested in your thoughts about the change, how you see it will affect Xavier High School, your classroom, and your teaching. The interview will take about 45 minutes. There *is a form requiring your signature noting you are participating in the interview*.

2   All faculty and staff are being interviewed over a two-week period. The information will be compiled, aggregated, and presented at a full faculty meeting; you will have all the information we have collected. All the data will be ANONYMOUS, you, individually, will not be identified in any way. This is a method called SURVEY DATA FEEDBACK, and is often used to collect information so that everyone knows the *collective* opinion of a faculty. From this information the faculty should be able to see what issues and concerns

need to be addressed. If the information is to be truly representative of the Xavier faculty, it is important that you are forthright with your opinions and thoughts.

3   I will be taking notes as we talk. We are also using a tape recorder for back-up purposes.

4   Do you have any questions for me before we begin?

As we continue with our study, we would appreciate follow-up input on the transition and change to coeducational schooling at Xavier. Please complete the following survey.

Age
male/female
Are you a religious or lay person?
How many years have you taught?
How many years have you taught at Xavier?
What is your present assignment?

Teacher:
Math/Science
English/Languages
Religion
Social Science
P.E./Health

Non-teacher:
Administration
Staff, what?
Other

1   First, will you describe your own educational background? Where did you go to school? To college? Where have you taught?

2   What attracted you to teach at Xavier High School?

The following section addresses changes at the school, in your *teaching*, and in the *classroom*. As you respond, think about the three levels: school, your teaching, and classroom. First, about school.

3a   Xavier High School will become a coeducation school next fall. What, in your opinion, will change at Xavier High School? *Be as specific as possible – give examples.*

3b   Do you see these changes as positive, negative, or neutral? (Add +, –, 0 by each change indicated, to give some indication about the changes.)

4   Please describe your teaching – your philosophy, the methods you use, the outcomes you want for students. Be as specific as possible.

5   Beginning next fall, coeducational classrooms will begin at Xavier. Will this affect your teaching? Will your philosophy, methods, outcomes differ? Why or why not? (Indicate whether these changes are +, –, 0.)

6   Now think about the classroom. Beginning next fall, with boys and girls in classrooms, think of the classroom environment. Will coeducational classrooms change the environment of the classroom? Again, please indicate whether you see these changes as +, –, or 0.

7   At this time what are your expectations and concerns about coeducational schooling, in the school, the classroom, or your own teaching?

8   What can be done to facilitate the transition to coeducational schooling? Are there things that could assist you, individually, with the transition?

9   Thinking about your readiness to move to coeducational schooling, how ready are *you*? If 1 indicates Not Ready and 10 indicates you are Very Ready, where are you on the scale?

Not Ready   1   2   3   4   5   6   7   8   9   10   Very Ready

Why do you place yourself there?

10   Thinking about the Xavier faculty's readiness to move to coeducation, how ready do you think they are? If 1 indicates Not Ready and 10 indicates the faculty are Very Ready, where are the Xavier faculty on the scale?

Not Ready   1   2   3   4   5   6   7   8   9   10   Very Ready

Why did you place the faculty there?

11   Is there anything you would like to add to this survey?

Appendix B
Xavier Faculty Follow-Up Questionnaires

Questionnaire for Xavier Faculty

April 25, 1994

To: Xavier Faculty

From: The Research Team

This questionnaire is a follow-up of our interviews last spring. We hope all of you will answer the questions. It should take about 20 minutes.

We have asked for names so we can match these responses to your previous interview. ALL RESPONSES WILL BE CONFIDENTIAL; WE WILL IMMEDIATELY REMOVE NAMES AND ATTACH A CODE NUMBER TO YOUR QUESTIONNAIRE. NO INDIVIDUALS WILL BE IDENTIFIED.

Name:

Department:

Indicate the *approximate number* of men/women in each of class:

Class name	No. men	No. women	Grade level
Class name	No. men	No. women	Grade level
Class name	No. men	No. women	Grade level
Class name	No. men	No. women	Grade level
Class name	No. men	No. women	Grade level

1   THINKING ABOUT XAVIER HIGH SCHOOL AS A WHOLE what were TWO major surprises you experienced with the change to coeducation during the 1993–1994 school year?

2   THINKING ABOUT YOUR OWN TEACHING (e.g. curriculum, pedagogy) what were the TWO major issues you experienced with the change to coeducation during the 1993–1994 school year?

3   THINKING ABOUT YOUR CLASSROOMS (e.g. social dynamics, discipline, student responses) what were the TWO major issues you experienced with the change to coeducation during the 1993–1994 school year?

4   Change always creates surprise. What was ONE SURPRISE that you experienced with the change to coeducation during the 1993–1994 school year?

5   As you prepare for the second year of coeducation at Xavier High School, what are TWO issues/concerns/problems that need to be addressed?

6   Last spring we asked about the faculty's "readiness" to teach in coeducational classrooms, individually and collectively. This spring we ask about "ableness" (ability, competence).

a   How able are you, INDIVIDUALLY, to teach male and female students in the same classroom? Please circle one:
Not Able   1   2   3   4   5   6   7   8   9   10   Able

b   How able do you see your colleagues (in the school as a whole) to teach both male and female students in the same classroom? Please circle one:
Not Able   1   2   3   4   5   6   7   8   9   10   Able

7   Concerning our research on coeducation/single-sex schools, what do you wonder about? What issues would you like the research team to address?

Questionnaire for New Xavier Faculty Members

April 25,1994
   To: New Xavier Faculty Members
   From: The Research Team
   This questionnaire will assist us in our research on coeducational/single-sex schools. It should take about 20 minutes.
   We have asked for names and departments. ALL RESPONSES WILL BE CONFIDENTIAL; WE WILL IMMEDIATELY REMOVE NAMES AND ATTACH A CODE NUMBER TO YOUR QUESTIONNAIRE. NO INDIVIDUALS WILL BE IDENTIFIED.

Name:
   Department:
   Indicate the *approximate number* of men/women in each of class:

Class name	No. men	No. women	Grade level
Class name	No. men	No. women	Grade level
Class name	No. men	No. women	Grade level
Class name	No. men	No. women	Grade level
Class name	No. men	No. women	Grade level

1   THINKING ABOUT XAVIER HIGH SCHOOL AS A WHOLE, what were TWO major surprises you experienced coming to Xavier High School as a new faculty member?

2   THINKING ABOUT YOUR OWN TEACHING, what were TWO major *issues* you experienced in teaching coeducational classes?

3   THINKING ABOUT YOUR CLASSROOMS (e.g. social dynamics, discipline, student responses) what were the TWO major issues you experienced in coeducational classes at Xavier?

4   As you prepare for the second year of coeducation at Xavier High School, what are TWO issues/concerns/problems that need to be addressed?

5   Concerning our research on coeducation/single-sex schools, what do you wonder about? What would you like the research team to address?

Appendix C

Guiding Questions for the Xavier Faculty Focus Groups, February, 1994

General focus

Last spring, each faculty, administrator, and staff member outlined his or her expectations and concerns regarding the transition to coeducation. This morning we want to understand how these expectations and concerns played out in reality. What has happened and not happened to Xavier and to your teaching as a result of the move to coeducation?

What effect has the presence of young women had on

School climate for learning
The school culture of Xavier
Discipline, roles, and codes of conduct
Student development (social, moral, and intellectual)
Your philosophy of teaching?

What aspects of coeducation have been positive, which have been negative, and why?

What did you *not* anticipate about the impact of coeducation on Xavier school?

Describe the young women as learners and as adolescents. Does this match your anticipation about girls as students at Xavier?

Appendix D
Student Surveys

Student Survey, 1993

To: Xavier Students

Your insights about the change to a coeducational school are important. We appreciate your responses on this survey. Please circle your responses to each question.

Please circle your current class at Xavier.

Freshman / Sophomore / Junior / Senior

1 Having girls at Xavier next year will change the school atmosphere.
not at all / somewhat / very much

2 I am looking forward to attending Xavier with girl students.
not at all / somewhat / very much

3 Teachers will teach differently when girls are in the classroom.
not at all / somewhat / very much

4 Teaching will be better when girls come to Xavier.
not at all / somewhat / very much

5 The social environment at Xavier will change next year.
not at all / somewhat / very much

6 Having girls in the classroom will make it easier to get good grades.
not at all / somewhat / very much

7 Opportunities to become good friends with guys will change when girls enter Xavier.
not at all / somewhat / very much

8 Having girls come to Xavier is a good idea.
not at all / somewhat / very much

9 What are your greatest concerns about the addition of girls to Xavier?

10 Do you wish that Xavier would remain an all-male school? Why or why not?

Student Survey, 1994

To: Xavier Students

We appreciate your responses on this survey. Please circle your response to each question.

Please circle your current class at Xavier.

Freshman / Sophomore / Junior / Senior

What school did you attend last year?

Please indicate your gender: Female / Male

1 Compared to my school experience last year, I think the school atmosphere this year is different.

not at all / somewhat / very much

2 Compared to my school experience last year, teachers teach differently now.

not at all / somewhat / very much

3 Compared to my school experience last year, I think teaching has improved.

not at all / somewhat / very much

4 Compared to my school experience last year, I think the social environment has changed.

not at all / somewhat / very much

5 Compared to my school experience last year, I think opportunities to become good friends with members of my sex have increased.

not at all / somewhat / very much

6 Compared to my school experience last year, I think opportunities to become good friends with members of my sex have decreased.

not at all / somewhat / very much

7 Compared to my school experience last year, I think opportunities to become friends with members of the other sex have increased.

not at all / somewhat / very much

8   Compared to my school experience last year, I think opportunities to become friends with members of the other sex have decreased.
   not at all / somewhat / very much

9   Additional comments

Appendix E
Student Focus Group Topics

Decision to attend your school:

Leadership
Social/peer relationships
Students' views of faculty and staff
Sports and extra-curricular activities

References

Angus, L. B. (1993). "Masculinity and women teachers at Christian Brothers College." *Organization Studies, 14*(2), 235–260.

Arnot, M. (1982). "Male hegemony, social class and women's education." *Journal of Education, 164*(1), 64–89.

Ashton, P. T. and Webb, R. B. (1986). *Making a difference: Teachers' sense of efficacy and student achievement.* New York: Longman.

Bandura, A. (1982). "Self-efficacy mechanism in human agency." *American Psychologist, 37*(2), 122–137.

Barba, R. and Cardinale, L. (1991). "Are females invisible students? An investigation of teacher–student questioning interactions." *Schools Science and Mathematics, 91*(7), 306–310.

Bauch, P. A. (1989, March). "Single sex schooling and women's education." Paper presented at the annual meeting of the National Catholic Educational Association, Chicago, IL.

Beacom, A. (1994). [Sadker Intersect Instrument classroom observation.] Unpublished raw data.

Belenky, M. F., Clinchy, B. M., Goldberger, N. R., and Tarule, J. M. (1986). *Women's ways of knowing: The development of self, voice and mind.* New York: Basic Books.

Bieler, R. (1984). *Science and gender: A critique of biology and its theories on women.* New York: Pergamon Press.

Bohmer, S. and Briggs, J. L. (1991). "Teaching privileged students about gender, race, and class oppression." *Teaching Sociology, 19*, 154–163.

Brody, C. (1993, April). "Co-teaching, teacher beliefs and change: A case study." Paper presented at the annual meeting of the American Educational Research Association, Atlanta, GA.

—— (1998). "The significance of teacher beliefs for professional development and cooperative learning." In C. Brody and N. Davidson (eds.), *Professional development for cooperative learning: Issues and approaches* (pp. 25–48). Albany, NY: SUNY Press.

Brody, L. and Fox, L. H. (1980). "An accelerative intervention program for mathematically gifted girls." In L. H. Fox, L. Brody, and D. Tobin (eds.), *Women and the mathematical mystique* (pp. 163–178). Baltimore: Johns Hopkins University Press.

Bryk, A., Lee, V., and Holland, P. (1993). *Catholic schools and the common good.* Cambridge, MA: Harvard University Press.

References

Buetow, H. A. (1988). *The Catholic school: Its roots, identity and future*. New York: Crossroads.

Burk, M. (1998, July/August). "NOW invokes Title IX to fight an all-girls school." *MS, 9*, 24–25.

Burnett, R. E. and Ewald, H. R. (1994). "Rabbit trails, ephemera, and other stories: Feminist methodology and collaborative research." *Journal of Advanced Composition, 14*(1), 21–51.

Campbell, P. B. (1995). "Redefining the 'girl problem in mathematics.'" In W. G. Secada, E. Fennema, and L. B. Adajian (eds.), *New directions for equity in mathematics education* (pp. 225–241). New York: Cambridge University Press.

Campbell, P. J. and Grinstein, L. S. (1988). *Mathematics education in secondary schools and two-year colleges: A sourcebook*. New York: Garland.

Casey, K. (1996). "The new narrative research." In M. W. Apple (ed.), *Review of research in education: Vol. 21* (pp. 211–254). Itsaca, IL: F. E. Peacock.

Cibulka, J., O'Brien, T., and Zewe, D. (1982). *Inner city private elementary schools: A study*. Milwaukee, WI: Marquette University Press.

Clark, C. M. and Peterson, P. L. (1986). "Teachers' thought process." In M. C. Wittrock (ed.), *Handbook of research on teaching* (3rd ed.) (pp. 255–296). New York: Macmillan.

Coleman, J. and Hoffer, T. (1987). *Public and private high schools: The impact of communities*. Reading, MA: Addison-Wesley.

Collins, P. H. (1990). *Black feminist thought: Knowledge, consciousness, and the politics of empowerment*. Boston: Unwin & Hyman.

Crosby, F. (1984). "The denial of personal discrimination." *American Behavioral Scientist, 27*(3), 371–386.

Cuban, L. (1988). "Constancy and changes in schools, 1880s to the present." In P. Jackson (ed.), *Contributing to educational change: Perspectives on research and practice* (pp. 85–106). Berkeley, CA: McCutcheon.

Dale, R. R. (1969). *Mixed or single sex schools: A research study about pupil–teacher relationship: Vol. 1*. London: Routledge & Kegan Paul.

—— (1971). *Mixed or single sex schools: Some social aspects: Vol. 2*. London: Routledge & Kegan Paul.

—— (1974). *Mixed or single sex schools: Attainment, attitudes and overview: Vol. 3*. London: Routledge & Kegan Paul.

Delpit, L. (1995). *Other people's children: Cultural conflict in the classroom*. New York: New Press.

Denzin, N. (1989). *Interpretive biography*. Newbury Park, CA: SAGE.

Dick, T. P. and Rallis, S. F. (1991). "Factors and influences on high school students' career choices." *Journal for Research in Mathematics Education, 22*(4), 281–292.

Dossey, J. A., Mullis, I. V. S., Lindquist, M. M., and Chambers, D. L. (1988). *The mathematics report card: Are we measuring up? Trends and achievement based on the 1986 National Assessment*. Princeton, NJ: Educational Testing Service.

Doyle, W. and Ponder, R. A. (1977). "The practicality ethic in teacher decision making." *Interchange, 8*, 1–12.

Dunlap, D. and Schmuck, P. (eds.) (1995). *Women leading in education*. Albany, NY: SUNY Press.

Eccles, J. and Blumenfeld, P. (1985). "Classroom experiences and student gender: Are there differences and do they matter?" In L. Wilkinson and C. Marrett (eds.),

Gender influences in classroom interaction (pp. 79–114). Orlando, FL: Academic Press.

Edmonds, R. (1979). "Effective schools for the urban poor." *Educational Leadership, 37*(1), 15–24.

Edson, C. H. and Schmuck, P. (1992). [Review of the book *Learning together: A history of coeducation in American public schools.*] *Educational Studies, 23*(2), 159–164.

Feeney, S. (1997). "Shifting the prism. Case explications of institutional analysis in nonprofit organizations." *Nonprofit and Voluntary Sector Quarterly, 26*(4), 489–508.

Felker, R. (1993). "The gestalt of a women's high school: 'Greater than the sum of its parts.'" In D. K. Hollinger and R. Adamson (eds.), *Single-sex schooling: Proponents speak: Vol. II* (pp. 27–37). Washington, DC: Office of Research, U.S. Department of Education.

Fennema, E. and Carpenter, T. P. (1981). "Sex-related differences in mathematics: Results from the National Assessment." *Mathematics Teacher, 74*(7), 554–559.

—— (1998). "New perspectives on gender differences in mathematics: An introduction." *Educational Researcher, 27*(5), 4–5.

Fennema, E., Carpenter, T. P., Jacobs, V. R., Franke, M. L., and Levi, L. W. (1998). "A longitudinal study of gender differences in young children's mathematical thinking." *Educational Researcher, 27*(5), 6–11.

Finn, J. (1980). "Sex differences in educational outcomes: A cross-national study." *Sex Roles, 6*(1), 9–26.

Fonow, M. M. and Cook, J. (1991). "Back to the future: A look at the second wave of feminist epistemology and methodology." In M. M. Fonow and J. Cook (eds.), *Beyond methodology: Feminist scholarship as lived research* (pp. 1–15). Bloomington: Indiana University Press.

Fowlkes, D. L. (1992). *White political women: Paths from privilege to empowerment.* Knoxville: University of Tennessee Press.

Frazier, N. and Sadker, M. (1973). *Sexism in school and society.* New York: Harper & Row.

Fullan, M. (1991). *The new meaning of educational change.* New York: Teacher's College Press.

Fuller, K. (1997). "With boys or without them: Exploratory study of math education for girls." Unpublished doctoral dissertation. Stanford University, Palo Alto, CA.

George, H., Jr. (1906). *The menace of privilege: A study of the dangers to the republic from the existence of a favored class.* New York: Macmillan.

Gilligan, C. (1982). *In a different voice.* Cambridge, MA: Harvard University Press.

Goffman, E. (1959). *The presentation of self in everyday life.* New York: Doubleday Anchor.

Gosetti, P. P. (1995). "Gender privilege: A case study of an all male Catholic high school transitioning to coeducation." Unpublished doctoral dissertation. University of Oregon, Eugene.

Hafernik, J. J., Messerschmitt, D. S., and Vandrick, S. (1997). "Collaborative research: Why and how?" *Educational Researcher, 26*, 31–35.

Haller, E. (1985). "Pupil race and elementary school ability grouping: Are teachers biased against Black children?" *American Educational Research Journal, 22*(4), 254–265.

References

Hallinen, M. (1981). "Recent advances in sociometry." In S. R. Asher and J. M. Gottman (eds.), *The development of children's friendship* (pp. 91–115). Cambridge, MA: Harvard University Press.

Harding, S. (1987). "Introduction: Is there a feminist method?" In S. Harding (ed.), *Feminism and methodology* (pp. 1–14). Bloomington: Indiana University Press.

—— (1991). *Whose science? Whose knowledge? Thinking from women's lives.* Milton Keynes, UK: Open University Press.

Hiller, C. (1998). "Dis/Locating gendered readings: Moving towards a critical pedagogy of estrangement." Unpublished doctoral dissertation. University of Tasmania, Tasmania, Australia.

Hilliard, A. G. (1988). "Conceptual confusion and the persistence of group oppression through education." *Equity and Excellence, 24*(1), 36–43.

Hollingsworth, S. (1994). *Teachers' research and urban literacy education: Lessons and conversations in a feminist key.* New York: Teacher's College Press.

Hord, S., Rutherford, W., Huling-Austin, L., and Hall, G. (1987). *Taking charge of change.* Alexandria, VA: Association for Supervision and Curriculum Development.

Hyde, J. S. and Jaffee, S. (1998). "Perspectives from social and feminist psychology." *Educational Researcher, 27*(5), 14–16.

Jansen, S. C. (1989). "Gender and the information society: A socially structured silence." *Journal of Communication, 39*(3), 196–215.

Kenway, J. and Willis, S. (1986). "Girls, self-esteem and education: From the personal to the political and from the universal to the specific." Paper presented at the AARE Conference, Melbourne, Australia.

—— (1997). *Answering back: Girls, boys and feminism in schools.* New South Wales, Australia: Allen & Unwin.

Klein, S. S. and Ortman, P. E. (1994). "Continuing the journey toward gender equity." *Educational Researcher, 23*(8), 13–21.

Lather, P. (1991). *Getting smart: Feminist research and pedagogy within the postmodern.* New York: Routledge.

Leder, G. C. (1992). "Mathematics and gender: Changing perspectives." In D. A. Grouws (ed.), *Handbook of research on mathematics teaching and learning* (pp. 597–622). New York: Macmillan.

—— (1995). "Equity inside the mathematics classroom: Fact or artifact?" In W. G. Secada, E. Fennema, and L. B. Adajian (eds.), *New directions for equity in mathematics education* (pp. 209–224). New York: Cambridge University Press.

Lee, V. E. (1997). "Gender equity and the organization of schools." In B. J. Bank and P. M. Hall (eds.), *Gender, equity and schooling: Policy and practice* (pp. 135–158). New York: Garland.

Lee, V. E. and Bryk, A. S. (1986). "Effects of single-sex secondary schools on student achievement and attitudes." *Journal of Educational Psychology, 78*(5), 381–395.

—— (1988). "Curriculum tracking as mediating the social distribution of high school achievement." *Sociology of Education, 61*, 78–94.

Leithwood, K., Begley, P., and Cousins, B. (1992). *Developing expert leaders for future schools.* Bristol, PA: Falmer Press.

LePore, P. C. and Warren, J. R. (1997). "A comparison of single-sex and coeducational Catholic secondary schooling: Evidence from the National Educational

Longitudinal Study of 1988." *American Educational Research Journal, 34*(3), 485–511.

Lewis, M. and Simon, R. I. (1986). "A discourse not intended for her: Learning and teaching within patriarchy." *Harvard Educational Review, 56*(4), 457–472.

Lincoln, Y. S. and Guba, E. G. (1985). *Naturalistic inquiry.* Beverly Hills: SAGE.

Lockheed, M. E. (1985). "Sex equity in classroom organization and climate." In S. Klein (ed.), *Handbook for achieving sex equity through education* (pp. 189–217). Baltimore, MD: Johns Hopkins University Press.

Lockheed, M. and Hall, K. P. (1976). "Conceptualizing sex as a status characteristic: Applications to leadership training strategies." *Journal of Social Issues, 32*, 111–124.

Lyons, N. P., Saltonstall, J. F., and Hamner, T. J. (1990). "Competencies and visions: Emma Willard girls talk about being leaders." In C. Gilligan, N. P. Lyons, and T. J. Hamner (eds.), *Making connections: The relational worlds of adolescent girls at Emma Willard School* (pp. 183–214). Cambridge, MA: Harvard University Press.

Maccoby, E. and Jacklin, C. (1974). *The psychology of sex differences.* Palo Alto, CA: Stanford University Press.

Maher, F. and Tetreault, M. K. (1994). *The feminist classroom.* New York: Basic Books.

Marsh, H. W., Owens, L., Meyers, M. R., and Smith, I. D. (1989). "The transition from single-sex to co-educational high schools: Teacher perceptions, academic achievement, and self-concept." *British Journal of Educational Psychology, 59*, 155–173.

Marsh, H. W., Smith, I. D., Marsh, M. R., and Owens, L. (1988). "The transition from single sex to coeducational high schools: Effects on multiple dimensions of self-concept and on academic achievement." *American Educational Research Journal, 25*(2), 237–269.

Marshall, C. (1997). *Feminist critical policy analysis. Vol. 1: The primary and secondary school perspective.* London: Falmer Press.

Martin, J. (1992). *Cultures in organizations: Three perspectives.* New York: Oxford University Press.

McArthur, E. (1995). *Use of school choice* (NCES Publication No. 95–742). Washington, DC: U.S. Government Printing Office.

McIntosh, P. M. (1988). "White privilege and male privilege: A personal account of coming to see correspondences through work in women's studies." Working Paper No. 189, Wellesley College, Center for Research on Women, Wellesley, MA.

Miles, M. (1983). "Unraveling the mystery of institutionalization." *Educational Leadership, 41*(3), 14–19.

Miller, J. (1976). *Toward a new psychology of women.* Boston: Beacon Press.

—— (1986). *Toward a new psychology of women* (2nd ed.). Boston: Beacon Press.

Morgan, G. (1986). *Images of organization.* Newbury Park, CA: SAGE.

Murphy, P. and Gipps, C. (eds.) (1997). *Finding equity in the classroom.* Melbourne, Australia: Falmer Press and UNESCO.

Nagel, N., Brody, C., and Pace, G. (1994, April). "What will change? Issues in transition from a single-sex school to a coeducational school." Paper presented at the annual meeting of the American Educational Research Association, New Orleans, LA.

References

National Catholic Educational Association (NCEA) (1985). *The Catholic high school: A national portrait*. Washington, DC: Author.

National Council of Teachers of Mathematics (NCTM) (1989). *Curriculum and evaluation standards for school mathematics*. Reston, VA: Author.

—— (1991). *Professional standards for teaching mathematics*. Reston, VA: Author.

—— (1994). *Voices of change in mathematics education*. Reston, VA: Author.

National Science Foundation (NSF) (1990). *Women and minorities in science and engineering*. Washington, DC: Author.

Noddings, N. (1998). "Perspectives from feminist philosophy." *Educational Researcher, 27*(5), 17–18.

Noffke, S. E. (1997). "Professional, personal, and political dimensions of action research." In M. Apple (ed.), *Review of research in education: Vol. 22* (pp. 305–343). Washington, DC: American Educational Research Association.

Oakes, J. (1985). *Keeping track: How schools structure inequality*. New Haven: Yale University Press.

—— (1990). *Multiplying inequalities: The effects of race, social class, and tracking on opportunities to learn mathematics and science*. Santa Monica, CA: The Rand Corporation.

Office of Educational Research and Improvement (OERI) (1992, March). *Working meeting on single gender schooling*. Washington, DC: Author.

Orenstein, P. (1994). *Schoolgirls: Young women, self-esteem, and the confidence gap*. New York: Anchor Books.

Proweller, A. (1998). *Constructing female identities*. Albany, NY: SUNY Press.

Reinharz, S. (1992). *Feminist methods in social research*. New York: Oxford University Press.

Richardson, V. P., Anders, P., Tidwell, D., and Lloyd, C. (1991). "The relationship between teachers' beliefs and practices in reading comprehension instruction." *American Educational Research Journal, 28*(3), 559–586.

Riggs, I. (1988). "A review of factors related to gender and ethnic differences in math/science achievement levels of K-12 students." *Educational Considerations, 15*(1), 18–21.

Riordan, C. (1990). *Girls and boys in school: Together or separate?* New York: Teacher's College Press.

Rosener, J. B. (1990). "Ways women lead." *Harvard Business Review, 68*(6), 119–125.

Rusch, E. A. and Marshall, C. (1995, April). "Gender filters at work in the administrative culture." Paper presented at the annual meeting of the American Educational Research Association, San Francisco, CA.

Sadker, M. and Sadker, D. (1994). *Failing at fairness: How our schools cheat girls*. New York: Charles Scribner's Sons.

Sadker, M., Sadker, D., and Klein, S. (1991). "The issue of gender in elementary and secondary education." In G. Grant (ed.), *Review of research in education: Vol. 17* (pp. 269–334). Washington, DC: American Educational Research Association.

Schein, E. (1985). *Organizational culture and leadership*. San Francisco: Jossey-Bass.

Schmuck, P. (1995). "Advocacy groups for women administrators." In D. Dunlap and P. Schmuck (eds.), *Women leading in education* (pp. 199–224). Albany, NY: SUNY Press.

Schmuck, P., Brody, C., Fuller, K., Gosetti, P. P., Pace, G., Nagel, N., and Moscato, S. (1996, November). "Doing feminist research on gender in a Catholic male high school becoming coeducational." Paper presented at the annual meeting of the American Educational Research Association's Special Interest Group: Research on Women in Education, San Jose, CA.

Schmuck, R. (1997). *Practical action research for change*. Arlington, IL: IRI, Skylight.

Schmuck, R. and Schmuck, P. (1996). *Group process in the classroom* (8th ed.). Dubuque, IA: William C. Brown.

Schulz, R., Schroeder, D., and Brody, C. M. (1997). "Collaborative narrative inquiry: Fidelity and the ethics of caring in teacher research." *Qualitative Studies in Education, 10*(4), 473–485.

Secada, W. G., Fennema, E., and Adajian, L. B. (eds.) (1995). *New directions for equity in mathematics education*. New York: Cambridge University Press.

Shmurak, C. (1998). *Voices of hope: Adolescent girls at single sex and coeducational schools*. New York: Peter Lang.

Sleeter, C. E. (1993). "Power and privilege in white middle-class feminist discussions of gender and education." In S. K. Biklin and D. Pollard (eds.), *Gender and education: Ninety-second yearbook of the national society for the study of education* (pp. 221–240). Chicago: University of Chicago Press.

Smith, D. E. (1987). *The everyday world as problematic*. Boston: Northeastern University Press.

Sowder, J. T. (1998). "Perspectives from mathematics education." *Educational Researcher, 27*(5), 12–13.

Stallings, J. (1979). *Factors influencing women's decisions to enroll in advanced mathematics courses: Executive summary*. Menlo Park, CA: SRI International.

Stanic, G. M. A. and Hart, L. E. (1995). "Attitudes, persistence, and mathematics achievement. Qualifying race and sex differences." In W. G. Secada, E. Fennema, and L. B. Adajian (eds.), *New directions for equity in mathematics education* (pp. 258–278). New York: Cambridge University Press.

Strauss, A. and Corbin, J. (1994). "Grounded theory methodology: An overview." In N. K. Denzin and Y. S. Lincoln (eds.), *Handbook of qualitative research* (pp. 273–285). Thousand Oaks, CA: SAGE.

Streitmatter, J. (1998). *For girls only: Making a case for single sex schooling*. Albany, NY: SUNY Press.

Streitmatter, J., Blair, H., and Marasco, J. (1996, April). "Girls only classes in public schools." Paper presented at the annual meeting of the American Educational Research Association, New York.

Stromquist, N. (1997). "Gender policies in American education: Reflections on federal legislation and action." In C. Marshall (ed.), *Feminist critical policy analysis: A perspective from primary and secondary schooling* (pp. 54–72). Washington, DC: Falmer Press.

Style, E. (1988, June). "Curriculum as window and mirror." Paper presented at the Conference on Listening for All Voices: Gender Balancing the School Curriculum, Oak Knoll School, Summit, NJ.

Tannen, D. (1990). *You just don't understand*. New York: Ballantine Books.

Tetreault, M. K. (1986). "The journey from male-defined to gender-balanced education." *Theory into Practice, 25*, 227–234.

Tetreault, M. K. and Schmuck, P. (1985). "Equity, educational reform and gender." *Issues in Education, 3*(1), 45–67.

References

Tirrell, L. (1993). "Definition and power: Toward authority without privilege." *Hypatia, 8*(4), 1–34.

Tyack, D. and Hansot, E. (1990). *Learning together: A history of coeducation in American schools*. New Haven, CT: Yale University Press.

Wasser, J. D. and Bresler, L. (1996). "Working in the interpretive zone: Conceptualizing collaboration in qualitative research teams." *Educational Researcher, 25*(5), 5–15.

Weiler, K. (1988). *Women teaching for change: Gender, class and power*. New York: Bergin & Garvey.

Willingham, W. W. and Cole, N. S. (1997). *Gender and fair assessment*. Mahwah, NJ: Lawrence Erlbaum Associates.

Willis, S. and Kenway, J. (1986). "On overcoming sexism in schooling: To marginalize or mainstream." *Australian Journal of Education, 10*, 132–149.

Women on Words and Images (1972). *Dick and Jane as victims: Sex stereotyping in children's readers*. Princeton, NJ: Author.

Wong, D. E. (1995). "Challenges confronting the researcher/teacher: Conflicts of purpose and conduct." *Educational Researcher, 24*(3), 22–28.

Zanders, A. (1993). "A presentation of the arguments for and against single-sex schooling." In D. K. Hollinger and R. Adamson (eds.), *Single-Sex Schooling: Proponents Speak, Vol. II* (pp. 15–20). Washington, DC: Office of Research, U.S. Department of Education.

Notes on the Authors

Celeste M. Brody is Associate Professor of Teacher Education at Lewis and Clark College in Portland, Oregon, where she specializes in instructional theory, models for groupwork, adult development, integrated curriculum, and field-based master's programs. She co-edited with James Wallace, *Ethical and social issues in professional education* (SUNY, 1993), and with Neil Davidson, *Professional education for cooperative learning: issues and approaches* (SUNY, 1998). Her research interests include collaborative, narrative inquiry, cooperative learning, and teacher cognition.

Kasi Allen Fuller received her Ph.D. in Educational Administration and Policy Analysis from Stanford University in 1997. She currently works from her home as an educational consultant and evaluator for a variety of programs funded by the National Science Foundation. Her present research interests include: reform in K-12 mathematics and science education, issues of equity, and teacher professional development.

Penny Poplin Gosetti is Assistant Professor of Higher Education Administration in the Department of Educational Leadership at the University of Toledo in Toledo, Ohio, where she teaches courses in research, college student personnel administration, and student development theory. Her interest in the areas of gender equity and privilege, organizational culture, and learning environments intertwines her perspectives gained as a higher education administrator, with her research in secondary school settings.

Susan Randles Moscato, RN, EdD is Associate Professor at the University of Portland School of Nursing, Portland, Oregon, where she teaches research utilization and leadership and coordinates the senior nursing practicum. Her areas of interest include research on power and change, patient outcomes, and community development strategies.

Nancy G. Nagel is Associate Professor of Education at Lewis and Clark College in Portland, Oregon, where she coordinates an elementary preservice cohort and teaches elementary school mathematics. She also works with teachers in the area of integrating curriculum. For the past ten years, she has directed mathematics and/or science education grant projects. She is author of *Learning through real-world problem solving: The power of integrative teaching* (Corwin, 1996) and co-author of *Early childhood education: The world of children, families, and educators* (Allyn & Bacon, 1999). Research interests include teaching and learning in mathematics, gender issues, and preservice education.

Glennellen Pace is Associate Professor of Education in the field of language and literacy at Lewis and Clark College, Portland, Oregon, where she coordinates an elementary cohort in the preservice master of arts in teaching program. Her research interests include literacy acquisition and development, and the impact of school reform issues on the pedagogical practices of classroom teachers.

Patricia Schmuck received her MA from the University of Michigan and Ph.D. from the University of Oregon. Currently a Senior Scholar, she is a former Professor of Educational Administration at Lewis and Clark College, Portland, Oregon. She is the author/co-author/editor of numerous articles and books in education. Books include: *Women leading in education*, with co-editor Diane Dunlap, *Group processes in the classroom*, with co-author Richard Schmuck, which is in eight editions and four languages. Her academic work involves democracy in education, women in administration, and gender. She is recently retired, and spends time tending her large garden overlooking Mt Hood and working as a volunteer with service agencies for young women.

Index